Statistics and Data Analysis for

SOCIAL WORKERS

JOHN L. CRAFT
University of Iowa

with the assistance of
LAWRENCE R. ASKLING

F.E. PEACOCK PUBLISHERS, INC.
ITASCA, ILLINOIS 60143

Copyright © 1985
F.E. Peacock Publishers, Inc.
All rights reserved
Printed in the U.S.A.
Library of Congress
Catalog Card No. 84–061422
ISBN 0-87581-305-4

Preface

This book is about the use of numbers in social work and other human service professions. It is designed to present basic statistical concepts directly applicable to the types of analytical problems encountered by social workers and others.

This book is intended for undergraduate and graduate students in social work and related disciplines. For several years students have requested a book written "just like you present it and explain it in class." This book is an attempt to honor those requests. The authors' classroom experience and work with human-service agencies over the years have clearly indicated that workers and administrators need a text that will help them understand and interpret the data generated by themselves and others in the delivery of human services.

We are deeply indebted to the scores of social-work students at the University of Iowa who have provided encouragement for and helpful criticism of the content of the book. They are truly "co-authors." A special debt of gratitude is due Dixie Kramer, who spent many hours skillfully translating the authors' handwritten narrative into the final product. We are grateful to John F. Else for his many helpful criticisms and suggestions.

We are especially grateful to Joyce Usher and Linda Pierce of F. E. Peacock Publishers, Inc., for their thoroughness, diligence and general positive demeanor throughout the preparation of this book.

Special thanks go to Tom Walz, who has contributed to the authors' professional and personal development in so many ways, many of which are not measurable by the statistical techniques presented in this book.

This book is dedicated to the memory of our friend and buddy, Bill Sackter. In his unique way Bill taught us and countless others the true meaning of love, compassion, and friendship. We are truly richer for having known him and shared his life.

I am grateful to the Literary Executor of the late Sir Ronald A. Fisher, F.R.S. to Dr. Frank Yates, F.R.S. and to Longman Group Ltd, London for permission to reprint Tables 8.1, 8.2 and 8.4 from their book *Statistical Tables for Biological, Agricultural and Medical Research* (6th Edition, 1974).

We are especially grateful to our wives, Marty and Jan, for their help, understanding, and sharing their lives with us. Their tolerance and encouragement have been very important to us.

JOHN L. CRAFT
LAWRENCE R. ASKLING

Dedicated to the memory of Bill Sackter
"How Sweet It Is!"

Contents

Chapter 1

Introduction

The focus of this book is on the analysis and interpretation of data generated by social workers in practice. Social-work practice involves a variety of decision-making levels and activities, from policy making, planning, and administration (macro-practice) to direct-service intervention (micro-practice) with individual clients. Social work practice involves continual decision making and research skills are an important and integral part of sound decision making.

Quality decision making requires that judgments be formed on the basis of good information. Social work research is concerned with the systematic collection, analysis, and interpretation of information for input into the decision-making process. Social work research can be considered a tool to aid the practitioner and policy maker in making the best informed decisions possible. The methods of social work research guide the production of practice-relevant information; the methods of social work practice determine how the information is utilized.

The research conducted in social work can be characterized by its diversity in both methods used and the investigators who use these methods for carrying out their inquiries. Social work research is noted for its eclectic nature in choosing a method or methods to investigate a particular problem.

Much of what we consider as social work research is carried out in the practice setting by practitioners themselves. These information gathering and analyzing activities are often applied in nature and limited in scope. Other social work research involves more extensive investigations, either in terms of time and effort invested in the study or in terms of the particular research design and data-analysis techniques employed.

University-based research conducted by social work faculty and students (latent practitioners) has grown markedly in the last decade. Some of the research done in the academic setting is directly related to practice concerns and some to more theoretical issues. University researchers (including students) often work hand in hand with caseworkers, supervisors, planners, and administrators within agency settings in investigating and obtaining solutions to both short-range and long-range problems faced by these practicing professionals. Rather than maintain an artificial dichotomy between social work research and social work practice, it is becoming more and more recognized that social workers today can comfortably deal with both; thus, the term practitioner/researcher is now widely used to denote the integration of the two aspects of the social-worker role.

The social work research process is a multi-stage process that involves problem formulation, choosing an appropriate research design, devising data collection instruments, data collection, and data analysis and interpretation. The content of this book is concerned primarily with the data analysis and interpretation stages of the research process. This is not to say that the earlier stages are less important. Excellent readings are available on the logic of research, research designs, instrument construction, ethical considerations in conducting research, and other important research issues. But, unless social workers have a good understanding of what they can and should do with data once they have them, knowledge of methods and techniques for producing data lead them only part way to the end of the research maze. Social workers can and should use an in-depth understanding of data analysis as a guide in the selection and application of various research methods and techniques. So in our discussions here we will assume that the data under perusal were gathered while taking into account these other important research considerations. We will then begin from that point to see how we can better analyze and understand the data generated from our data-collection efforts.

Before we begin our journey through the labyrinth of data processing and analysis, it will be helpful to set the context or framework within which social work research is carried out.

Our primary interest in this book is to provide aid to the social worker in practice. We shall concentrate our topical presentations and discussions on those concepts and techniques that we feel are most important and useful in analyzing the kinds of information (data) that social workers deal with in action. Our goal is to help social workers learn how the appropriate use of statistical analysis will in turn help them make better sense out of the myriads of information surrounding them on a regular basis.

In doing social work research (broadly defined), social workers sometimes collect information on what are termed *samples,* and at other times on what are called *populations.* Sometimes these terms become confused. Both terms refer not only to people or events *per se,* but also rather to a collection of measurements made on these people or events. Thus, a population is a set of measurement scores on a defined number of people or events under study. If we are interested in studying all of the clients that receive services during a one-year period at a particular agency, then by definition the measurements on the clients over this one-year period are our population of scores. A *sample* is merely a subset of scores from the larger population of scores. If we picked one half of the clients from the one-year period, then this would be a *sample* of scores derived from the population of scores from the total one-year period.

Whether we consider a set of scores to be a sample or population of scores depends in part on what the investigator intends to do with the outcome from an analysis of the data. If our interest is only in describing and interpreting a set of scores (data) that we have *in hand,* then we use *descriptive statistics.* The data can be considered as coming from either a sample or a population. The distinction is not useful in this case.

However, if our intent is to use this set of data in hand to try to understand an even larger body of data, then we apply *inferential statistics* on the sample data and make estimates about the characteristics of a larger body of data (population data). We will return to the concepts of samples and populations of scores at several points in this book.

As the preceding discussion indicates, social-work "researchers" today carry out their activities in a variety of settings, picking from a fairly extensive selection of research methods and techniques. Social workers use a variety of techniques to collect information (data) about clients, families, other workers, agencies, and communities. These include data derived from client-case research, agency records, questionnaires, interview schedules, management-information systems (MISs), and census data. Once a set of data is in hand, the social worker needs a large array of statistical tools available to aid in organizing, summarizing, describing, interpreting, and presenting the data. The objective is to use these tools to help expand the knowledge base and aid in improving delivery of service.

The following chapters detail what these tools are and when and how they can be used. The outcome will be the ability to do a complete *descriptive* analysis of a set of data, including frequency distributions; measures of central tendency, dispersion, and relative standing; measures of association and correlation; and communication of data by tables and graphs. Further, you will learn how to use a few of the more common tests of statistical significance. Real data from a variety of social work research efforts are used throughout the book to present the concepts and procedures.

Quite often we have a computer available to help us with our data analyses. If we are really fortunate, we have an experienced computer programmer attached to the computer. However, many times we have only a hand calculator at our disposal to aid with our computations. And, sometimes, we have just a pencil and paper. In any case, it is useful and even intrinsically pleasing to do some of the calculations while learning to use the variety of statistical procedures and techniques presented in this book. By doing some of the calculations, we get a "feel" for the data, as well as an understanding of what the procedures do and when they are appropriate to use. And, of course, after we have done several calculations, we will come to appreciate more fully just how valuable a computer is as an analytic aid.

Many students start a course in social work research and data analysis with either an abhorrence or trepidation of numbers (or both) and anything or anyone associated with them. Quite often these negative feelings die and are replaced by positive feelings of accomplishment and appreciation. The following simple numerical exercises are introduced to help rehearse some fundamental mathematical manipulations. To many students these exercises will appear to be banal or just plain simple. Of course, you are entitled to your opinion, and we respect your right to object. But after you are through sneering, *work the exercises anyway, for there is method in our madness.* Everything we do has a purpose.

PROBLEMS

1. List the numbers 21 through 30, inclusive, in a single column on a piece of paper. Write in a second column the *number of times* each of the following numbers (21 through 30) occurs:

29	25	21	26	30
24	29	23	27	26
24	30	29	27	28
21	28	27	26	27

2. Which number in problem 1 appears most often? least often?

3. In the following list there is one number that is greater than three of the others but also less than three of the others. What is the number?
    313; 98; 101; 7; 3613; 69; 25

4. There is a number, let us call it M, which is equal to your age plus the ages of two of your friends, divided by 3. Calculate the value of M.

5. Subtract 9 from each of the following numbers, being careful to watch the sign of the remainder.
    13; 14; 4; 8; 5; 10
    Now square each of the remainders and add the squares; that is
    $$(13\text{-}9)^2 + (14\text{-}9)^2 + (4\text{-}9)^2 + (8\text{-}9)^2 + (5\text{-}9)^2 + (10\text{-}9)^2 = ?$$

6. Now divide the answer to problem 5 by 6 and take the square root of the quotient. Use a calculator or table of square roots.

7. Add the following numbers and square their sum: 2; 4; 6; 8; 10. This may be written as $(2+4+6+8+10)^2$.

8. Square each of the following numbers and add their squares: 2; 4; 6; 8; 10. Once you have done this, compare your answer to the answer to problem 7, and you will see that the *square of the sum* (problem 7) does not equal the *sum of the squares* (problem 8).

9. Arrange the following numbers in order from greatest to least:
    35; 17; 2; 14; 21; 7; 11
    Rank these seven numbers by assigning a 1 to the greatest number, a 2 to the next greater number, and so on until you assign a 7 to the least number.

10. Add the following set of numbers: 22; 24; 26; 28. Divide the sum by 4. Call this quotient A. Then add 10 to each of the four numbers, and again divide by 4. Call this quotient B. How does B compare with A?

11. Now divide 22, 24, 26 and 28 each by 2, then add the quotients, and then divide by 4. Call this result C. How does C compare with A in problem 10?

12. We assume you have worked each of the eleven problems and found them enjoyable. Those of you who meet our assumption have performed every single mathematical operation and applied many of the formulas used in this text. You are to be commended. You are now ready to enter the remaining chapters of the book. Before you start, a word of warning! You must remember not to lug dirt to a hilltop.

Chapter 2

The Nature of Data

When we do a descriptive analysis of a set of data, we say we are *doing* descriptive statistics on the data, or we are *using* descriptive statistics on the data.

But what are these data to which we are applying all of these statistical procedures? We will define data as a set of numbers that represent categories or instances of variables. How we get and assign these numbers is a basic issue we will address shortly. But, first we will present two examples of the types of data with which social workers might be involved.

Table 2.1 presents a portion of a data set generated from a social work research project. The project is concerned with collecting information about persons who use the services of domestic-violence shelters in a midwestern state; it is part of an ongoing agency information system used to analyze and evaluate the agency's clientele and services.

What do we see when we look at Table 2.1? At first glance, all we see is a large set of numbers that appear to be meaningless. What do these numbers represent? Where did they come from? What do they tell us about shelter clients? We will have to do something to this set of numbers that will help us impart meaning to the numbers.

The numbers in Table 2.1 represent responses to a large number of questions asked of a sample of fifteen shelter clients. All responses were coded to numerical form for statistical analyses. One set of responses from one client is referred to as one *case*. Table 2.1 contains numerically coded responses from 15 cases. The first two lines (rows) contain responses from case 1. The next two lines are data from case 2, and so on through case 15. Each question in this context is called a *variable*. This study involved obtaining data related to 117 different variables. Thus, the data set in Table 2.1 contains numerically coded information on 117 variables for 15 cases.

Table 2.2 contains a small sample of data obtained from a central child-abuse registry in a midwestern state. The original data are generated by child-protective service workers who fill out a reporting form for each of their cases.

TABLE 2.1. Selected data from a study of domestic-violence shelters

```
13252111  2212421652   86 8 66      1115  164121 3  1111121212
11222222221122122            322222221 22222221412221 5    222212
132951 121 22111263121               1115511             21222221
12222211211222222 12221222321 22222222221221   5   211123
13252111   12211115511566      3111155 163122 1 21111122212
11112211221112221 112222121121 222222221 2222262221 22
131721111311211121631346416111111  111336163132 1121121222221
121222221222222121211121112221 222222221 2222122 192222112 2212221
12282121 1222   21  112 1       241114   153 31 1111121221211
11112211221122121 12221222212221 2122      2242122112 3212221
122121112 22233222112 1         3311134 144132 1121111222222
121222222221212222 2      312222222      124222113223212221
122421222112211 12112 666      2 1213  161172 2 22221222211
12222221212      11122222122222222221122 3154 211222211221
1224212121112211121112 46   24     1 14  1431221 221212212222
121222221212121221112122222222212 22222      235231211221211222
122822 2114122211341136  666666 211124  12512111211111221222
12222221122      142222221 121211212122122223222121111211221
0420212121222  216612 66 6 66      521114  1   222 1121111221221
1222222221      151222122212221 2222      1202222 22 1222212
04392121212221111621171        3211177 162272 1221111111212
1222222122 12222122212222221221 2222      149212 15111223221
1249212121112212222256111444      2 1116  152142 1221211221221
2222221211      1111222222 12222122      1502121 22 222221
123221 2 122215213511362 2      3111155 12317112 11121221222
12222221222      1 122112222121222222      1262222 52 2212221
12221121  21211113111362 8 28  3211111 141112 1 21111121222
111222111211112221411222212211211222222221 221221122211111211221
12322121 221212111511566      21216  162 21111222211221222
1121221112121112213111122222211222222      13122 211112211222
```

These are sent to a central office where the numerically coded information is entered into a computer for analysis. The analyses of these data are used by department staff for planning and allocation of resources.

What do the numbers in Table 2.2 tell us about child abuse in this midwestern state? Without further information, very little or nothing. What we must do is apply certain statistical procedures to the numbers to see what information they contain about child-abuse cases.

Once again, the information obtained about one client is called one case. Table 2.2 contains numerically-coded information on 34 variables for a sample of 40 child-abuse cases. Note in Table 2.2 that it only requires one line

TABLE 2.2. Selected data from a central child-abuse registry

```
040 518792 1   1 7211 21431003108 534416403931000 11
723 52179016   1 9613 20732003 86 325 3 26  33000150
790 52979011 199922 31331003178 764416343743000 16
240 6 579014 4899913161731201180112221645553     28
070 61279010   1 4813 20531030  0 334426303500000  3
900 61379010   1 2625 21031000130 41  16435100000  3
140 615790 5   1 6723 20831000170 424 2 40  00000  5
773 61879010   3 4813 20031 00170 513312212101000 12
780 6 179014   2 9613 20732000170 314 6 24  10100 10
570 6 779016 22 9411 21331003178 45  5      03000  9
773 61979016 7299933 20332000200 523 1 29  00000  6
770 62279012   4 6821100512000162 414 4 32        6
083 62279016999  731 20232000211 512222265242122  7
083 62279016999  741 20032000211 512222265242100  7
780 52979015   2 4511 21431000120 444 6 40  00000  3
780 6 879010   3 9633120832002137 91 222273442105 13
771 62179015 5699933 20942000170 413 6 40  00000  7
901 62279016   1 9111 10831000218 543316253400000 10
770 62279224 60 8721 21031000190 634426353500000  9
551 6 779011   7 2943 20532003201 713316333443003 32
551 6 779011   7 2953 20431003201 713316333443003 32
821 61179011   1 2421 203320  170 45        00000  5
425 521790 9   6 9633 20031002171 444416232433000  5
170 614790 9   1  823 20532003106 3    30  12000  5
220 52979016   1 7211 11632062104 422266505130010 24
780 61879010   1 2623 20831000170 76781 4353500000  5
780 620790 9   3 4833 20531000160 434 5 32  00000  4
780 62879014   1 9613 20931000200 534416282900000 17
821 7 279015   1 2333 20232000190 5        00000  1
820 7 3790 9   3 4823 21131000170 8        00000  2
290 7 679016   1 2453 101320   210 73336634350     3
820 62779220   1 2411 20632000170 8        00000  7
090 62979015   1  713 20631100106 414466212430100  5
090 7 079011   1 2911 21632000218 474466404043000 10
090 7 279011   1 2921 21531000218 474466404043000 10
780 61879011   3 9623 20832000200 335456303100000 12
400 62379219   1 7214 51531003178 654314363631000  7
771 7 179222999 9111 10031000198 3133111734       7
07  7 579011   1  412 11632000101 314414424342100  6
775 62979012 52 7423  0631000208 623316322710100 11
```

to represent the information obtained from each of the 40 cases. In Table 2.1 two data lines were necessary for each of the 15 cases.

What do the numbers in Table 2.2 stand for? The first two numbers in each line indicate the county in which the child-abuse report was filed. The 26th and 27th numbers depict the perpetrators of the abuse. The 23d and 24th numbers (columns 23 and 24) show the age of the child. In a similar fashion, the remaining numbers in each line represent the categories of the remaining 31 variables, such as year of the report, type of service offered, sex of the child, and so on. It should be pointed out here that the 40 cases in Table 2.2 are only a small sample from a population of approximately 70,000 cases reported over a four-year period.

Now that we have seen some examples of numbers that make up a data set, it is necessary to take a closer look at how the numbers were obtained and what numerical meaning can be attached to them.

MEASUREMENT AND LEVELS OF MEASUREMENT

In the process of collecting data relevant to social work, we typically measure more than one variable at a time. A *variable* is some observable entity, object, or event that can take on more than one characteristic or value. These different characteristics or values that variables take on are often referred to as the categories of variables. The biological sex of people is a variable. Male and female are categories or instances of this variable. Age of people is a variable. The various years are categories of this variable. Type of counselling—individual, family, or group—is a variable. The three types of counselling listed are categories of this variable.

As is true with other professions and disciplines, social work practice is replete with variables. In fact, it is the delineation and study of sets and classes of variables that serve to help provide identity for a particular profession or discipline. It is the study of these variables and the linkages among them that foster the advancement of knowledge. Measurement plays a key role in this enterprise.

Recording an observation is known as *measurement*. Measuring a variable involves assigning values or symbols to observed instances or categories of a variable, according to specified rules. The rules that define the assignment of an appropriate value determine the *level of measurement* for a particular variable. The different levels are defined on the basis of the ordering and distance properties inherent in the measurement rules. These rules are very important because which particular statistical technique one should use on data depends, in large part, on at which level the data is measured.

There are four types or levels of measurement to be considered. For analytical purposes these four levels will usually involve the assignment of numerals to observed variables. Some variables take on fairly prescribed values, such as the variable age and number of service hours. Other variables take on less obvious values and often require an arbitrary coding scheme to identify various categories adequately. Variables of this type include marital status and ethnicity.

Nominal Measurement

The nominal level of measurement is sometimes called the qualitative level and is the simplest form of measurement. The word *nominal* is derived from the Latin word for name, *nomine*. Hence, nominal measurement involves the assignment of names to the various categories of variables. We are primarily interested in the assignment of numeral names to variable categories. For example, instead of naming people as married, single, or divorced, we can name these categories of the variable marital status 1, 2, or 3. Or we can label them 5, 6, or 7. It is important here that we not consider these numeral names as numbers. We can perform neither arithmetic nor logical operations on data measured at the nominal level. Nothing is implied about the relationships that might exist among different categories. We must remember that at the nominal level of measurement, 1, 2, 3, and 4 are not numbers, they are numerals. But because nominal measurement is simple, does not mean it is of little use. In many situations, nominal-level statistics are the only appropriate measures to use. We will see evidence of this in the following chapters.

Ordinal Measurement

Ordinal measurement allows us to rank objects, events, and people according to some quality. Classifying people as low, moderate, or high in self-esteem implies that there is an ordering among the three categories. Assume we assign the numerals 1, 2, and 3 to these categories. Then people who fall in category 3 are judged to possess more self-esteem than those in category 2. Similarly, those in category 2 possess a higher level of self-esteem than those in category 1. What we have done is simply ranked people into these categories. Therefore, we know that there is a "distance" or interval between categories, but we do not know what that distance is. We can neither add these categories to one another nor perform other mathematical operations on them. But having our variable-categories rank ordered does give us a higher level of measurement than simply naming or labeling the categories.

Interval and Ratio Measurement

It is at the interval level of measurement that we can begin to perform arithmetic operations on data. Interval numbers have magnitude because they are based on a common unit of measurement. This means that the distance from one number to its adjacent number is equal to the distance from any other number on the continuum to its adjacent numbers. We say that such numbers are along an *equal-interval scale*.

Consider three people with self-esteem scores of 25, 35, and 45. First of all, these people are classified into one of three self-esteem categories (nominal). Second, the scores follow in order along the dimension (ordinal). If we consider the difference between 25 and 35 units of self-esteem to be equal to the self-esteem difference between 35 and 45, then we are placing the variable self-esteem on a scale or dimension with equal intervals. We have thus measured the variable self-esteem along an interval scale. Measuring variables on an interval scale allows one to perform the operations of addition and subtraction on the numbers on the scale.

The *ratio level* is distinguished from the interval level in that ratio scales of measurement have an absolute zero. An absolute zero point for a measurement scale means that there is a point on the scale where none of the variable being measured exists. Commonly occurring ratio scales are the several physical measurements: length, weight, and time. Other variables of interest that can be considered to be ratio level are income and family size.

In social work research the distinction between the interval and ratio levels is usually not important; the same statistic often is used for both levels.

Many social work research projects include the analysis of data measured at several levels of measurement. The data in Tables 2.1 and 2.2 include several variables at each of the levels of measurement. One of our goals in research is to obtain such precision of measurement that we can say we are studying variables that lie along at least an interval scale. This then enables us to use more sophisticated statistical techniques in our analysis of data. Some social workers (and others) would argue that measurement in social work research at best has reached the ordinal level. There are, however, those who contend that variables of a psychological or social nature most likely approximate interval measurement. Hence, these variables can be treated as if they were, in fact, interval-level scales. It may be a long and arduous task to "prove" that we have measured such concepts as self-esteem and group cohesiveness on an interval scale. In most cases, the game of proof may not be worth the candle. The position taken here is that it is often necessary and appropriate to consider some ordinal-level measurement as interval-level measurement. But it is important that we and others recognize the possibility of error in analysis and interpretation that may arise from doing so.

Chapter 3

Organization and Presentation of Data

Descriptive statistics are used to untangle a seemingly unorganized set of data, such as those in Tables 2.1 and 2.2, and to provide meaning to the data. The purpose of this chapter is to examine some of the basic techniques for organizing and presenting data. Throughout this book we stress the utility of data. For data and data analyses to be useful to the social work practitioner and administrator, the data must first be meaningfully organized and presented.

FREQUENCY DISTRIBUTIONS

One of the first things we can do with a set of data to facilitate comprehension is to organize the data into a set of frequency distributions, one distribution for each variable in the data set. If we have ten variables in a data set, we can

TABLE 3.1. Ages of children from small sample of child-abuse registry

14	07	09	16	06
07	13	08	08	16
13	03	10	05	15
17	05	05	09	08
05	02	04	02	15
10	00	03	11	00
08	14	00	01	16
00	08	05	06	06

construct as many as ten frequency distributions of the individual variables. If we have 50 variables in a data set, we can construct as many as 50 frequency distributions.

Table 3.1 presents the ages of the children from our small sample of 40 cases shown in Table 2.2. These ages are listed in columns 23-24 in Table 2.2. The first child in our list was reported as 14 years old and the last as 6 years old. A child listed as 0 years old means that this child is less than one year old.

What is the youngest age in our sample? How many are there of this age? What is the oldest age? the most frequent age? Do the ages bunch up at any part of the age continuum, or are the ages spread out? These are but a few of the questions we can ask to help us understand data such as these.

We could answer these questions by scanning the data in Table 3.1 several times. We can make our task easier, however, by providing some organization to the data. There are two basic formats we can use.

TABLE 3.2. Frequency distribution of sample age scores in descending order

Score (age)	f	Score (age)	f
17	1	8	5
16	3	7	2
15	2	6	3
14	2	5	5
13	2	4	1
12	0	3	2
11	1	2	2
10	2	1	1
9	2	0	4

Table 3.2 shows the ages organized in a descending fashion, from the highest age to the lowest. The ages are listed under the *score* heading. Each age is then called an age score. These "scores" are also called "codes" and are often merely symbolized with the letter "X." Thus, we can label our column of age categories as scores, codes, Xs, or merely with the name of the variable being distributed. The second column is labeled f for frequency, and the number in the column indicates how many times a particular score, code, or X category for a variable appears in the data. In our example here, the fs indicate how many times each of the listed age scores appears in our sample of 40 cases.

Table 3.3 shows the same age data distributed in an ascending manner as we go down the table. Which way we distribute the X scores is arbitrary; but since most computerized statistical procedures output frequency distributions with the Xs in ascending order, this is the convention we will follow. Note in Table 3.3 that constructing a frequency distribution of the 40 age scores allows us to determine quickly the lowest, highest, and more frequently occurring ages in the sample. The usefulness of organizing data into frequency

TABLE 3.3. Frequency distribution of sample age scores in ascending order

Score (age)	f	Score (age)	f
0	4	9	2
1	1	10	2
2	2	11	1
3	2	12	0
4	1	13	2
5	5	14	2
6	3	15	2
7	2	16	3
8	5	17	1

distributions becomes more evident as the number of cases we are studying increases.

The number of variable categories to use in a frequency distribution is usually placed between 6–15. More than this many categories or values of a variable listed make a frequency distribution almost as confusing as the original ungrouped data. We can reduce the number of age categories shown in Table 3.3 by grouping the age categories together as shown in Table 3.4. Table 3.5 shows the number of age categories reduced even further. Note that while reducing the number of categories makes reading the distribution table easier, the reduction results in the homogenization of the data, and distinctions between categories become blurred. In other words, we begin to lose some of the important details inherent in the data. A general rule of thumb is *to use at least six and not more than fifteen categories or intervals in a frequency distribution.* This rule assumes, of course, that you have at least six categories of a variable to begin with. Many variables used in social work research, such as client sex, ethnicity, marital status, and type of therapy are not represented by more than five categories. For these variables we present

TABLE 3.4. Grouped sample age scores

Score (age)	f	Score (age)	f
0–1	5	10–11	3
2–3	4	12–13	2
4–5	6	14–15	4
6–7	5	16–17	4
8–9	7		

all categories in our distribution and do not concern ourselves with grouping of categories or intervals.

Frequency distributions do a remarkable job of condensing large masses of data. Consider how much more difficult it would be to make meaning of data like those in Table 3.1 if the number of cases were increased. Table 3.6 contains a frequency distribution of the ages of 6,669 children reported as abuse and/or neglect victims.

TABLE 3.5. Sample age scores grouped into three categories

Score (age)	f
0–5	15
6–11	15
12–17	10

Inspection of Table 3.6 readily reveals that the most frequently reported age is 2, the least reported is 18, and children 5-years old or younger have the highest probability of being reported victims. It would be an impossible task to reach these same conclusions from a disorganized list of 6,669 individual ages. In fact, it would be difficult to reach any conclusion from such a listing. Note there are 19 age categories listed in Table 3.6. One could reduce the size of Table 3.6 by grouping the age categories into intervals. But, in this case a reduction may not serve any useful purpose.

RELATIVE FREQUENCIES AND CUMULATIVE FREQUENCIES

As we have seen, the second column in Table 3.6 indicates how many times (f) a given score (X) occurs in the distribution of scores. The third column in Table 3.6 expresses the frequency as a percentage of the total number of scores (N) in the distribution. This is called the relative frequency (Rf) of a particular X. For example, 501 of 6,669 children, or 7.5%, were four years old. Calculating percentages here involves dividing a given f by the total number of scores or cases. The frequency for the age category 10 is 324. This represents $(324/6669) \times 100$ or $.049 \times 100$, which equals 4.9%.

One reason we convert absolute frequencies to relative frequencies is that expressing parts as a fraction of a whole sometimes helps us comprehend and retain the nature of the frequency distributions. A more important reason for using relative frequencies is that they allow us to compare distributions within and between studies without the necessity of having equal Ns. Thus we can compare the age distributions of males and females and not be concerned whether or not the number of males and females is the same.

Cumulative frequencies (Cf) in percentage form are useful if we want to know the relative standing of a particular category in a distribution. A

TABLE 3.6. Frequency distribution of 6,669 age scores from child-abuse registry

Child's Age	Frequency f	Relative f in Percent	Cumulative f in Percent
0	421	6.3	6.3
1	555	8.3	14.6
2	607	9.1	23.7
3	533	8.0	31.7
4	501	7.5	39.2
5	455	6.8	46.1
6	404	6.1	52.1
7	391	5.9	58.0
8	352	5.3	63.3
9	339	5.1	68.3
10	324	4.9	73.2
11	264	4.0	77.2
12	305	4.6	81.7
13	311	4.7	86.4
14	300	4.5	90.9
15	252	3.8	94.7
16	220	3.3	98.0
17	124	1.9	99.8
18	11	0.2	100.0
	N=6669*	100.3**	

*Note: N is used to refer to the number of cases or scores in a distribution of cases or scores.
**Note: The relative frequency total does not add to 100% because of rounding by the computer routine.

cumulative f in percent for a given score (X) gives the percent of cases that take on *that value or less*. Table 3.6 shows that 404 cases are six years old. This represents 6.1% of all the cases (Rf). Furthermore, we know by looking in the cumulative-frequency column that 52.1% of the reported cases were six years old or younger and 90.9% of the children reported were 14 years old or younger. Of course 100.0%, or all, of the children were 18 years old or younger.

Presenting absolute frequencies and relative frequencies is appropriate for variables measured at any level: nominal, ordinal, or interval. The use of cumulative frequencies is not appropriate for variables measured at the nominal level.

Table 3.7 illustrates a frequency distribution of the sex of a child reported in an abuse/neglect case. Note first in Table 3.7 that the N is 6,701. For the ages distributed in Table 3.6, the N was 6,669. The difference in Ns is due to the sex of the child being reported for more cases than the age of the child. In other words, the age of the child was not reported for as great a number of cases as was the sex of the child. Missing data are a problem that seems to plague us

TABLE 3.7. Frequency distribution of sex of child from child-abuse registry

Sex of Child	f	Relative Freq.
Female (1)	3326	49.6
Male (2)	3375	50.4
	$N=6701$	100.0

when collecting data via reporting forms and questionnaires. For some variables we obtain complete information; for others we get data on a high percentage of cases; on still other variables the information is not available for many reasons and ends up being treated as missing data. As an example, the sex of the child in the child-abuse data set was reported for 98.6% of the cases (6,701 of 6,796 cases). Age was reported for 98.1% of the cases ($N=6,669$). However, occupation of the father was indicated for only 59.7% of the cases ($N=4,060$). Family income was reported for 88.9% of the cases.

Sex or gender is a nominal variable. Therefore the code values of 1 and 2 for female and male serve only as category labels. We could just as well have used the code 1 for male and code 2 for female. Or, we could have used numbers other than 1 and 2. The important thing to remember is that for most computerized data processing, we must convert nonnumeric-category labels to numeric labels, such as 1 and 2. Table 3.7 shows that the two sexes are nearly equally represented in the child-abuse reports, with a slightly higher percentage of the children being male. Also observe that it would not make sense in this case to report cumulative frequencies.

Table 3.8 presents a frequency distribution of family income reported for 6,045 of the child-abuse cases. First observe in Table 3.8 that the eight income categories on the child-abuse reporting form are coded 1 to 8. The income

TABLE 3.8. Family income distribution for 6,045 cases from child-abuse registry

Family Income (code)		f	Relative Freq.	Cumulative Freq.
Under 5,000	(1)	1799	29.8	29.8
5,000–7,999	(2)	1635	27.0	56.8
8,000–10,999	(3)	964	15.9	72.7
11,000–13,999	(4)	706	11.7	84.4
14,000–19,999	(5)	607	10.1	94.5
20,000–24,999	(6)	208	3.4	97.9
25,000–29,999	(7)	68	1.1	99.0
30,000–over	(8)	58	1.0	100.0
		$N=6045$	100.0	

scale 1 to 8 can be considered an ordinal scale but not an interval scale, since the size of the income intervals for the eight categories varies. If incomes were grouped into equal sized categories, then income would be an interval variable.

Table 3.8 shows that income category 1 occurred most often in the data (29.8%). Table 3.8 also shows that nearly three-fourths of the incomes (72.8%) were at income level 3 or below, or $10,999 or less. It would appear from these data that those families with lower incomes are more likely to be reported for child abuse/neglect. To determine how much more likely they are to be reported, one would have to compare this income distribution with an income distribution for a sample of all families in this midwestern state.

Frequency distributions provide a tabular form of presentation of how the various categories or values of a variable are distributed among the cases under study. Another manner in which these data may be presented is by using a graphical or pictorial representation of the distribution. Before we turn to graphs, however, it will be useful to present some more examples of tabular-frequency distributions. The data set we will use is the one resulting from the study of domestic-violence shelters. It was this data set we used to devise Table 2.1.

TABLE 3.9. Age distribution for domestic-violence shelter clients

Client Age	f	Rf	Cf
17	1	2.3	2.3
18	1	2.3	4.6
19	3	6.8	11.4
20	3	6.8	18.2
21	1	2.3	20.5
22	6	13.6	34.1
24	3	6.8	40.9
25	5	11.4	52.3
26	1	2.3	54.6
27	1	2.3	56.9
28	3	6.8	63.7
29	4	9.1	72.8
30	1	2.3	75.1
32	2	4.5	79.6
33	1	2.3	81.9
34	2	4.5	86.4
35	2	4.5	90.9
39	1	2.3	93.2
49	2	4.5	97.7
67	1	2.3	100.0
	N=44	100.0	

Table 3.9 displays the ages of 44 female clients of the domestic-violence shelters in this study. Note that the ages range from 17 to 67 and that several possible ages are not listed. These 44 women did not happen to be of those particular ages. Sometimes these values are included in the distribution and assigned a frequency of 0. If our sample size were increased, it is quite likely these other ages (e.g., 23) would start to occur in the age distribution.

Observe in Table 3.9 that the two most frequently occurring ages are 22 and 25. More than one half (52.3%) of the women are 25 years of age or younger. Three fourths are age 30 or younger. Does this mean that spouse abuse is more of a problem for younger women than for older women? Not necessarily. All we can conclude from these data is that younger women are more likely to be clients of domestic-violence shelters.

Table 3.10 shows the family income as reported by 37 of these clients. Once again, income as tabulated here should be considered an ordinal variable since the highest category has no upper limits. Well over one half of these families have an income of less than $5,000 per year. More than three fourths have an income of less than $10,000. This is a pattern similar to that observed for the child-abuse data presented in Table 3.8. Can we conclude that spouse abuse is more a problem for low-income than for higher-income families? Again, not necessarily, but it is suggestive. However, we can safely say that clients seeking service from domestic-violence shelters in this midwestern state are more likely to be from a lower-income family.

One more example of a distribution is in order. The frequency distribution presented in Table 3.11 is taken from a study of foster care in this same midwestern state. The study involved randomly selecting more than 400 foster-care cases and interviewing persons involved in either the delivery or receipt of these services. The data shown in Table 3.11 concern the type of placement into foster care, court ordered or voluntary. Note that cumulative frequencies were not included in the table since type of placement is a nominal variable. Table 3.11 clearly indicates that placement into the foster-care system in this state is predominantly through the legal system.

TABLE 3.10. Family income for domestic-violence shelter clients (n=37)

Income (code)		f	Rf	Cf
Less than $5,000	(1)	24	64.9	64.9
$5,000–9,999	(2)	5	13.5	78.4
$10,000–14,999	(3)	3	8.1	86.5
$15,000–19,999	(4)	1	2.7	89.5
$20,000 and over	(5)	4	10.8	100.0
		N=37	100.0	

TABLE 3.11. Type of Placement in foster care

Type of Placement (code)		f	Rf
Court Ordered	(1)	339	82.5
Voluntary	(2)	72	17.5
		N=411	100.00

COMPUTERIZED DATA PROCESSING

The frequency distributions discussed to this point were obtained from research studies of varying sample sizes, or Ns. A commonality of the studies is that each involved collecting data on a fairly large number of variables. These frequency distributions were not generated by laboring long and hard with a pencil and/or calculator. Rather, a widely used set of computerized data processing and analysis procedures were used. The particular computer package used was the Statistical Package for the Social Sciences, or as it is more commonly known, SPSSX. Most colleges and universities have access to these routines, as do many large agencies. Other statistical packages are also available for use.

The message here is that the advent of these easy to use sets of computer programs enables us as researchers to collect fairly large amounts of data and conduct a variety of analyses of the data and to do so in a rather painless manner.

An important point. In the main, our computers do no more nor no less than we instruct them to do. The fact that we can now readily use computers does not allow us to be less vigilant in paying attention to good-research design, appropriate sampling, and data-collection techniques. A computer cannot correct our mistakes nor our sloppiness in these areas. It merely inputs, processes, manipulates, analyzes, and outputs information. There are two ways you can remember this point. The first is GIGO, or garbage in, garbage out! The second is an old Japanese proverb—You cannot straighten a snake by passing it through a bamboo tube!

Now that we have seen how we can organize and condense data, we can turn to additional statistical tools and measures that we can use to help us and others understand the numerical fruits of our inquiries.

GRAPHICAL PRESENTATION OF DATA

The terms "chart" and "graph" are often used interchangeably, but they are not the same. Chart is the more generic of the terms and includes graphs, maps, posters, pictures, diagrams, and cartoons. Graphs are visual representations of numerical data that show distributions of data and reveal relationships existing between variables in the data. It is common to call a graph a figure, as we will do in the remainder of this book.

A major reason for using a graph is to present comparative, quantitative information quickly and simply. Graphs should be easy to read, and, therefore, should not be very complex. When a complex set of numerical data is to be portrayed, generally it is better to have a series of simple graphs rather than one intricate composite graph.

The basic nomenclature of a graph is shown in Figure 3.1. It is conventional to plot increasing values from left to right along the abscissa and to plot increasing values from bottom to top along the ordinate. Note that both axes start at the vertex, or the zero point. If our variable scale (e.g., age) or our frequency scale does not take on values of zero, or close to zero, then we usually "break" the axis by leaving a small piece missing, as is shown on the abscissa in Figure 3.1. Two other conventions are also important. We typically lay out our numerical scales along the axes so that most of the abscissa and ordinate are used. For the abscissa, we plot the lowest value of our scale near point A and the highest value near point B as in Figure 3.1. For the ordinate, the lowest and highest values are placed near points C and D. Another convention is to draw the ordinate approximately two thirds the physical length of the abscissa. If the abscissa is 6 inches in length, then the ordinate should be about 4 inches in length. Following these "rules of thumb" in terms of the structure of a graph is important. Not only are comparisons of data within and between studies made easier, but also there is less chance of

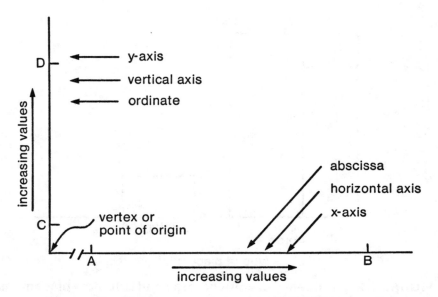

FIGURE 3.1. Diagram of graph nomenclature

data being distorted. By manipulating the length of axes and the scales plotted along the axes, we can make the same set of data say several different things.

Our discussion of graphs will focus on the graphing of frequency distributions. These are the most common uses of graphing in social work research. Generally speaking, different types of graphs are used, depending on the level of measurement for a particular variable.

Bar Graph

Bar graphs are used to display frequency distributions for nominal-level variables. Figure 3.2 displays the same data as was presented in tabular form in Table 3.11. The categories are labeled along the abscissa, and the height of the bar indicates the frequency of occurrence for each category. Since type of placement is a nominal variable, the bars do not touch. Also, because the assignment of numerals to the categories (1 and 2) was arbitrary, the relative location of the bars on the abscissa is arbitrary, that is, the locations can be reversed.

Histograms

A histogram is constructed by drawing bars whose width corresponds to category intervals of a variable and whose height corresponds to frequencies.

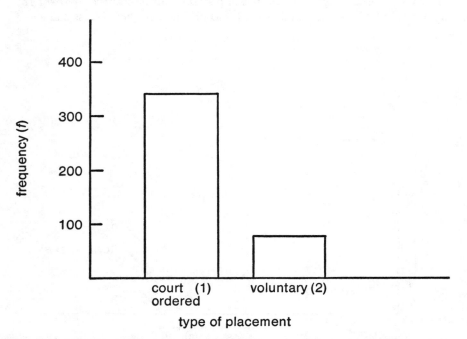

FIGURE 3.2. Frequency of court ordered and voluntary placement for 411 children in foster care

Histograms are appropriate for variables measured at the ordinal, interval, and ratio levels.

In graphic representations of frequency distributions an *area* is made to depict, or stand for, an individual score. We can then think of a column in a bar graph, or histogram, as being made up of individual scores that have been "melted" and "poured" to fill the columns. Another way to think of the column is as if the scores are "stacked" on top of each other in a column. In either case, each column represents the same number of scores as are shown in a tabular presentation of frequencies.

Figure 3.3 depicts a histogram of the same data shown in Table 3.10. The income intervals are labeled on the abscissa and the height of the columns indicates the frequency of occurrence of each income category. Since income is an ordinal variable, it is appropriate that the columns are adjacent to one another. Note how a graphical portrayal of these data more strikingly indicate the difference in the number of clients across income levels.

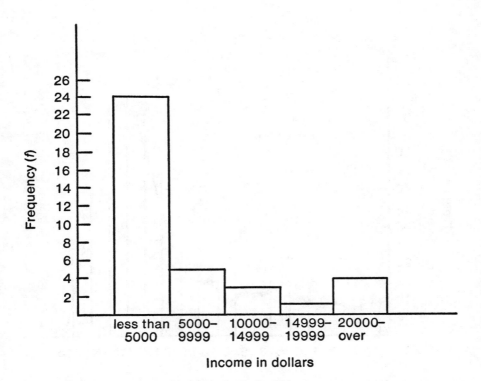

FIGURE 3.3. Family income for domestic-violence shelter clients (*N*=37)

Frequency Polygons

Another way to display how data are distributed is to present a frequency distribution in the form of a frequency polygon. A polygon is a closed geometric figure made by connecting many straight lines. A frequency polygon is a figure constructed from data in such a way as to create a graphic representation of those data. Actually, the frequency polygon is similar to the histogram, and one of these figures can be made from the other.

Figure 3.4 displays the age at first placement in foster care for 386 children in the foster-care study mentioned earlier. This graph shows a frequency polygon superimposed on a histogram depicting this frequency distribution. The polygon was constructed by making a dot in the center of the top of each column and then connecting the dots with straight lines. Figure 3.4 shows that the distribution of ages at first placement is concentrated at the upper end of the age scale.

Figure 3.5 presents a frequency polygon of the ages of child-abuse victims. These are the same data as those presented in Table 3.6. Note that the polygon

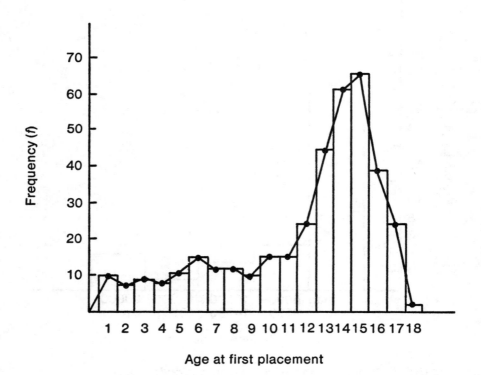

FIGURE 3.4. Age at first placement for 386 foster-care children

points are higher for the lower ages. This means that the ages of children reported as abuse/neglect victims are concentrated more at the younger ages. Frequency polygons and histograms are appropriate for pictorially displaying frequency distributions for variables measured at the ordinal, interval, and ratio levels. Which one should a researcher use to display data? For all practical purposes it is a matter of personal preference. Using graphs to present these frequency data allows one to determine the nature or shape of the distribution more readily than a tabular form of presentation does. The trade-off is that presentation precision is reduced by using graphs. That is, the actual frequency of occurrence for various categories is not always easily or precisely determined from graphs. Thus, whether one should use a graphical or tabular presentation of frequency data is dependent on the purpose of constructing the distribution in the first place. We will see in the next chapter how we can use graphs further to help us better understand and communicate the characteristics of our data.

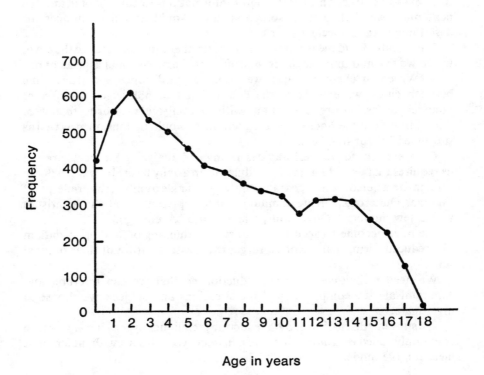

Age in years

FIGURE 3.5. Age distribution for 6669 children reported as abuse/neglect victims

Chapter 4

Data Reduction Techniques

The raw data products of our research efforts typically come to us in an unintelligible form. This was illustrated by the array of numbers presented in Tables 2.1 and 2.2. In Chapter 3 we discussed a few of the basic methods of reducing, organizing, and presenting data so that they become orderly enough to allow the extraction of meaningful information. In this chapter and the next ones, we shall present somewhat more sophisticated techniques for describing data in succinct forms.

Enumeration and measurement of all sorts of events characterize the era in which we live and impinge on both professional and personal aspects of our lives. We count client contacts; we measure the distance and travel time between cities; we enumerate the rise and fall of politicians in different political parties. We are so caught up with counting and measuring that, were it not for various methods of data reduction, we would be consumed as well as subsumed by our numbers.

Our penchant for numerically describing and analyzing the world around us requires that we indulge in data reduction on a daily basis. How often do we summarize a person's college transcript with a single number, the grade-point average? Quite often. How common is it to represent client characteristics with a few numbers? Often, but perhaps not often enough.

We have become so accustomed to seeing, thinking of, and using data in this reduced form, that we often forget the massive nature of their original state.

We need techniques for data reduction so that we can interpret and communicate the complexities of the situations and subjects we choose to investigate.

We start our discussion of data reduction techniques by looking at what are commonly called *measures of central tendency*. We will start with the simplest measure, the mode.

THE MODE

The mode of any distribution is the score or value that occurs with the greatest frequency. In the following distribution, 6 is the mode.

6 4 6 8 4 6 9

$X = 6$ has the greatest frequency of occurrence, that is, $f = 3$. It is therefore, by definition, the mode.

Many of the distributions with which we work in social work have the greatest concentration of scores near the *middle* of the range, or scale. Many distributions, however, have scores concentrated at either the lower ends or upper ends of the scale, or at both ends. In most instances, the score with the highest frequency, the modal score, coincidentally turns out to be somewhere near the portion of the scale where the scores are concentrated. Since this point may not be near the center of the scale, it is perhaps a misnomer to call the mode a measure of central tendency. It is more appropriately termed a measure of typicality.

A distribution may have more than one mode. If two variable values are tied in frequency, then the distribution for that variable is said to be *bimodal*. If a distribution has more than two modes, we usually say that it is *multi-modal*.

The mode or modes may usually be determined by inspection of a frequency distribution presented in either tabular or graphical form. If we are using a table form, we simply look for the score(s) with the highest f. If using a graphical form, we look for the high point(s) on the graph and then look down at the abscissa to read the score(s). It is important to point out here that a common error is to mistake the highest score (score of greatest magnitude) as the mode. Once again, the score occurring most frequently is the mode, no matter what its magnitude is. Table 4.1 is a tabular presentation of the foster-care study, age at first-placement distribution portrayed in Figure 3.4. A quick scan of the f or Rf column reveals that the modal age at first placement in foster care is 15 ($f = 66$ and R$f = 17.1\%$). One can also determine this quickly by inspection of Figure 3.4. Note that the mode in this case is not near the center of the range of ages. Hence, the preference for the term as a measure of typicality, rather than as a measure of central tendency.

THE MEDIAN

The median (Mdn) is an appropriate index of central tendency, since the median occupies a central position in any distribution, by definition. The median is that point along a continuum of scores below which (and above which) half the frequencies fall. The median occupies a central position by dividing a distribution into two parts, the upper 50% of all scores and the lower 50% of all scores. Consider the following simple example:

9
8
7
6
5

What is the median? The value 7.0 is the median. Picture the median as a very sharp razor blade that cuts the scores into equal halves. To do this, we must "slice" the distribution through the score of 7, leaving the values 5, 6, plus one half of 7 in the lower half, and the score 8, 9, plus the other half of 7, in the upper half. There are, then, 2½ scores on either side of 7.0, and 7.0 is, therefore, the median by definition.

COMPUTATION OF THE MEDIAN

For the computation of the median, it is necessary to introduce a concept called *real limits,* or *true limits,* for numbers.

Write your age on a piece of paper (not the book!). Let's assume you recorded the age of 25. Are you exactly 25, or are you 25 years, 6 months, 3 days, 2 hours, 9 minutes, and so on? Perhaps. Suppose someone else records the age of 25. Which of you is older? For most purposes, recording data in whole numbers or in integer form suffices. In other cases, we require more precision in our measurement.

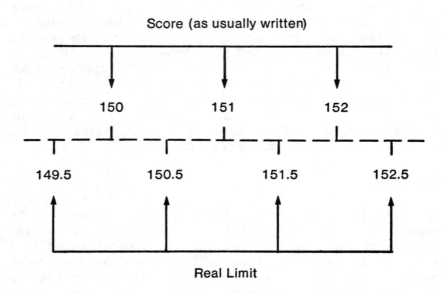

FIGURE 4.1. Diagram of location of real limits of a real set of numbers

In statistics, it is customary to record such variables as age in the same way that some insurance companies used to regard the age of their policy holders, to the *nearest* birthday instead of the last birthday. Thus, according to this scheme, any person between 24 years, 6 months old and 25 years, 6 months old is called 25 years old. When the person passes $25\frac{1}{2}$, the interval $25\frac{1}{2}$ to $26\frac{1}{2}$ is labeled with that interval's midpoint, 26. Using this rule, if someone's age is given as 25, all we know for sure is that the person is between $24\frac{1}{2}$ and $25\frac{1}{2}$ years old.

For our purpose, we will consider a score as extending over a range of $\frac{1}{2}$ *measurement unit below* and $\frac{1}{2}$ *measurement unit above* the score. The upper and lower limits of this range are called the *real limits* of that score. If we measure age in years, then the real limts for the age are $\frac{1}{2}$ year above and $\frac{1}{2}$ year below the age. If we measure weight in pounds, then the real limits for any weight are $\frac{1}{2}$ pound above and below the weight indicated by the scale. If someone has a weight of 151 pounds, then the lower and upper real limits for this score are 150.5 and 151.5, respectively. The idea is presented diagrammatically in Figure 4.1.

Note in Figure 4.1 that the upper real limit for one score is the lower real limit for the next highest score. Individual integer scores such as these are said to have an interval width of 1. If we group scores into intervals, such as 150 to

TABLE 4.1. Age at first placement foster-care study

Age (X)	f	Rf	Cf
1	10	2.6	2.6
2	8	2.1	4.7
3	9	2.3	7.0
4	8	2.1	9.1
5	11	2.8	11.9
6	15	3.9	15.8
7	12	3.1	18.9
8	12	3.1	22.0
9	10	2.6	24.6
10	15	3.9	28.5
11	15	3.9	32.4
12	24	6.2	38.6
13	45	11.7	50.3
14	62	16.1	66.3
15	66	17.1	83.4
16	39	10.1	93.5
17	24	6.2	99.7
18	1	0.3	100.0
TOTAL	386	100.1*	

*Note: The relative frequency total does not add to 100% because of rounding by computer routine.

152, then the real limits for this interval are 149.5 and 152.5. In grouped or ungrouped distributions, we can think of adjacent-score intervals as merging into one another. The interval width for any size interval actually extends from the lower to the upper real limits of the interval. The midpoint of an interval is the score that is half way between the values of the real limits. For interval widths of 1, or integer scores, the midpoint of the score interval is the score itself.

To find the median, we need to locate that point in a distribution of scores below which lie half of all the scores. Our task is greatly facilitated if we construct a frequency distribution of scores as in Table 4.1.

Observe in Table 4.1 that the *Cf* for an age score of 12 is 38.6%. This means that 38.6% of the ages, or 149 age scores, are less than 12.5, the upper real limit for the score of 12. The *Cf* for an age score of 13 is 50.3%. Thus, 50.3%, or 194 scores, are less than 13.5, the upper real limit for the score of 13. But we want to find that point, or median point, at which *exactly* 50.0% of the age scores are less in value than this median score. Since $N = 386$, we want the score that has 50% of 386, or 193, less in value. The 50% point, or median score, lies somewhere in the score interval 12.5 to 13.5.

There are 149 age scores less in value than 12.5. The interval 12.5–13.5 contains 45 age scores. It is important that we think of those 45 scores as being evenly spread out over the interval. To get a total of 193 scores ($\frac{1}{2}$ of N), we need 44 of the 45 scores in the interval. So we have to go 44/45 of the way into the interval, starting with the lower real limit of 12.5. Figure 4.2 diagrams this procedure. Since the interval width is 1-age unit, we need 44/45 of 1, or .978 of

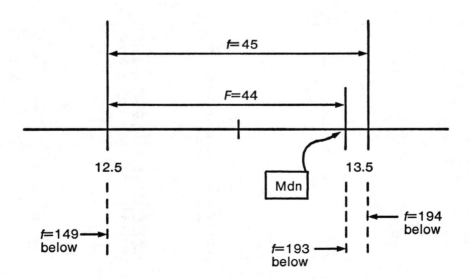

FIGURE 4.2. Diagram of procedure for determining median

the interval. We then add this amount to the lower real limit of the interval containing the median, or 12.5, and we have found the value of the median for this distribution of age scores. So,

$$\text{Median} = \text{Mdn} = 12.5 + .978 = 13.478$$

This obtained value, 13.478, is the precise value below which 50% of the age scores fall (and 50% above). This procedure can be captured nicely in the following formula:

$$Mdn = LRL + \left[\frac{\frac{1}{2}N - Cfb}{fw} \right] \times i$$

where Mdn = Median

LRL = lower real limit of interval containing Mdn

N = number of scores in distribution

Cfb = cumulative frequency *below* interval containing Mdn, or below LRL

fw = frequency within interval containing Mdn

i = width or size of interval containing Mdn

By using this formula, the completed equation would look like:

$$\text{Median} = 12.5 + \left[\frac{193 - 149}{45} \right] \times i = 12.5 + \left[\frac{44}{45} \right] = 12.5 + .978 = 13.478$$

Let us apply this formula to another distribution of scores to obtain the median. If we use the distribution of shelter-client ages shown in Table 3.9, we find by inspection of the Cf column that the interval containing the median is 24.5–25.5. We know this because 40.9% of the age scores are less than 24.5, but 52.3% are less than 25.5. So the 50% point (the median) is somewhere between these two values. Once again, we assume the 5 scores in the interval are spaced evenly over the interval.

$$\text{Median} = 24.5 + \left[\frac{22 - 18}{5} \right] \times i = 24.5 + \left[\frac{4}{5} \right] = 24.5 + .8 = 25.30$$

Thus, 50% of the ages are less than 25.30 in value, and 50% are greater in value.

THE MEAN

A more useful method of data reduction is the *mean,* or average, of scores. The type of average we are concerned with is the *arithmetic mean*. Although we don't use them often in analysis of social work research data, we should know that other means or averages do exist, namely the geometric and harmonic means. For our purposes, we will use the single term "mean," and know we are referring to the arithmetic mean.

So far in this chapter we have discussed concepts mainly in verbal terms.

We are at a point now where we must rely more on the use of symbolic terms. For example, as you are already aware, the mean (average) is computed by taking any collection of numbers, adding them, and dividing the sum by the number of numbers that were added. It is more efficient in terms of communication to reduce this verbal description of the mean to a set of symbols we have already used.

As you know, X is used to represent any score in a distribution. We have also used N to represent the number of individual scores in a distribution. The most common symbol used to represent the mean is $\bar{X}$ (read "ex-bar"). Using these three symbols, we can write a symbolic description of the mean as

$$\bar{X} = \frac{X_1 + X_2 + X_3 + \cdots + X_N}{N}$$

where $\bar{X}$ = the mean
  X_1 = the first score
  X_2 = the second score
  X_3 = the third score
  X_N = the last, or Nth, score
  N = the number of scores

The use of one more symbol, the Greek letter Σ, will help to shorten our symbolic description. The symbol Σ (upper-case sigma) signifies an operation to be performed, that of addition. If we say ΣX, this stands for "add the Xs." If we would say ΣX^2, this would stand for "add the X^2s." We add together that which appears to the right of the Σ. We can now write the description for the mean as:

$$\bar{X} = \frac{\Sigma X}{N}$$

where $\bar{X}$ = the mean
  Σ = the sum of
  X = each and every score
  N = the number of scores

This equation is called the raw-score equation for $\bar{X}$ and requires adding each and every score and then dividing by N. For short lists of scores, it is a simple process. For long lists of unordered scores, this can indeed be a laborious task. Since we often organize variable scores into frequency distributions, it is more efficient to compute the mean from the data contained therein.

Let us consider the problem of computing the average, or the mean, from the data in Table 4.1. We have already determined the mode and median for these age data. Remember that the numbers in the X column (in this case, ages) represent each *possible* score within the range, and that the numbers in the f column represent the number of *times* each of these scores occurred.

To compute the mean, we must find ΣX. One way to do this is to add in each score as many times as the number in the f column tells us it appeared in the original list of data. The age score of 1 would be added 10 times, the age score of 2 would be added 8 times, and so on. It may already have occurred to you that the sum of 8 individual 2s is the same as 8 multiplied by 2, since multiplication is a shortcut form of addition. If we multiply each X by its corresponding f, we can derive a series of subtotals, each representing the sum of all scores having the same value. We will call these subtotals fX (frequency times the score). We then modify our formula for the mean to

$$\bar{X} = \frac{\Sigma fX}{\Sigma f} = \frac{\Sigma fX}{N}$$

Apply these equations to the data in Table 4.1.

$$\bar{X} = \frac{(10 \times 1) + (8 \times 2) + (9 \times 3) + \cdots + (24 \times 17) + (1 \times 18)}{386}$$

$$= \frac{(10 + 16 + 27 + \cdots + 408 + 18)}{386} = \frac{4596}{386} = 11.907$$

Through the use of a frequency distribution, we have diminished the addition task necessary to compute $\bar{X}$ to the summing of only 19 numbers, the fXs. This is much simpler than summing 396 numbers. We could reduce our task even further by combining age scores into perhaps 5 or 6 intervals, but then we run the risk of losing the original identity of our scores. This also may result in error in calculation of the mean. We should note here a common error when computing the mean from a frequency distribution. You must remember to sum up the fXs (the frequencies times the scores) and *not* the Xs in a frequency distribution. Summing the Xs in this case and dividing by the number of different possible scores assumes that each score occurs with a frequency of 1. In Table 4.1 we found the mean to be

$$\bar{X} = \frac{\Sigma fX}{N} = \frac{4596}{386} = 11.907$$

The following shows how the error can easily be made:

$$\bar{X} = \frac{(1 + 2 + 3 + 4 + \cdots + 16 + 17 + 18)}{19} = \frac{171}{19} = 9.0$$

This error involves adding the possible ages and dividing by the number of possible ages, 19. It is obvious that 9.0 does not equal 11.907, the correct mean.

We have now determined by our data-reduction techniques that the modal age at first placement in the foster-care study is 15 years, the median age at first placement is 13.478 years, and the mean age at first placement is 11.907 years. We will see shortly what the differences between these measures of central tendency tell us about the shape of the distribution of age at first-placement scores.

First, though, let us work one more example of calculating the mean from a frequency distribution. Again using the data in Table 3.9 (ages of abuse-shelter clients), the mean is calculated as

$$\bar{X} = \frac{\Sigma fX}{N} = \frac{(17+18+57+\cdots+39+98+67)}{44} = \frac{1224}{44} = 27.818$$

Note that an fX column had to be created (not shown in Table 3.9) to compute the mean. The modal age for these shelter clients is 22 years, the median age we found to be 25.3 years, and our mean is 27.818. This pattern of magnitudes for Mo, Mdn, and $\bar{X}$ also indicates the probable shape of this age distribution, as we shall see.

WHICH MEASURE TO USE?

Inspection of the equation for the mean reveals that the value of the mean depends on the value of *each and every score* in the distribution of scores. The median value depends only on the value of those scores near the median. Extreme scores, either high or low, have no effect on the value of the median. The mode, of course, is affected only by the single value of the modal score, if the distribution is unimodal (one mode). If there is more than one mode, it is only these few score values that determine the mode(s).

Consider the following small set of ordered scores:

$$2, 3, 3, 5, 7, 8, 9, 9, 10, 12$$

There are two modes for these scores, 3 and 9. The median is 7.5 and $\bar{X}$ is 6.8. Let us change the score of 12 to 20. Our mean increases to 7.6, but the median and mode remain the same. If using the original 10 numbers, we change the 7 to 6, the mean decreases to 6.7, *and* the median decreases in value to 7.0. The mode remains the same.

The fact that the mean uses all of the scores in its determination is one reason it is the preferred of these three measures. If we repeatedly draw samples of scores from a larger population, we will find that the mean values vary less from each other than the median or modal values. This stability in value is very important when we attempt to estimate unknown population values from known sample values. The mean also enters into many statistical procedures used in both descriptive and inferential statistics, whereas the use of the median and mode beyond descriptive purposes is limited.

For distribution of scores that are unimodal and fairly symmetrical around the middle of the range of scores, the mean, median, and mode will be similar in value. Of the three, we prefer to use the mean. The mean, however, is not always the preferred measure of central tendency to use for descriptive purposes. As distributions deviate from symmetry around the midpoint, the mean becomes a less desirable score to use as a representative score. This will become clearer as we discuss in the next section how we measure and describe other characteristics of score distribution.

THE SHAPES OF DISTRIBUTIONS

It is quite possible you may have heard somewhere about the "normal"

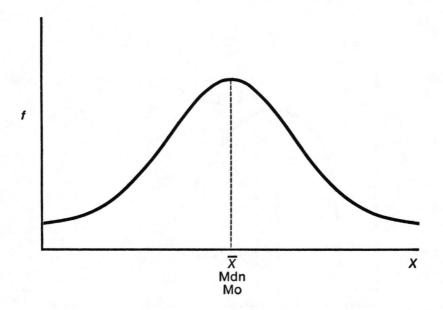

FIGURE 4.3. The normal curve

distribution, the "normal" curve, or the "bell-shaped" curve. To say that a distribution is "normal" identifies several characteristics of the distribution. First, the distribution is unimodal and symmetrical at the midpoint. Figure 4.3 shows a normal distribution. Observe that the mean, median, and mode all have the same score value in a normal distribution. By "symmetrical" we mean the right half of the distribution is the mirror image of the left half. Second, the *normal* probability curve is a graphic representation of a theoretical-mathematical distribution that will not be presented here. Many distributions of real measurements approximate closely a normal curve. We will discuss this more fully in the next chapter. It is important to remember now that when we form an image of frequency-distribution curves, the curves have a property of *density*. That is, the area under the curve and down to the abscissa is comprised of "stacks" or scores. We note that in a normal distribution, the scores are concentrated in and near the center of the range of scores.

If we have distributions with the highest frequencies at one end of the distribution rather than in the middle, these distributions are said to be *skewed.* Figures 4.4 and 4.5 are illustrations of skewed distributions. Figure

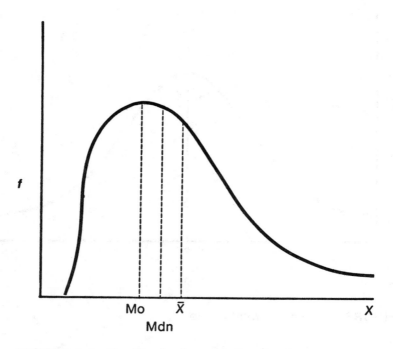

FIGURE 4.4. Positively skewed distribution

4.4 shows a *positively skewed* distribution. The scores are concentrated more toward the low scores, and the "tail" of the distribution points to the right, or in the "positive" direction. Figure 4.5 displays a *negatively skewed* distribution. Here the scores are concentrated more toward the high scores, and the tail points to the left, or in the "negative" direction. For example, an easy examination would produce a distribution of test scores that are negatively skewed. Most of the students would get high scores. A difficult examination would result in a positively skewed distribution of test scores. A few students would get high scores, but most would get lower scores. (We should point out that, for pedagogical purposes, we draw and present distributions that are "smoothed" out. These distributions rarely occur in real data.)

It is important to know whether a distribution is skewed or not, and to what degree. This knowledge helps us determine which measure of central tendency, the mean or median, to use in representing our data. Also, certain statistical procedures used for inferential purposes cannot be used if the score distribution(s) are markedly skewed.

There is a mathematical way of determining the degree of skewness that is

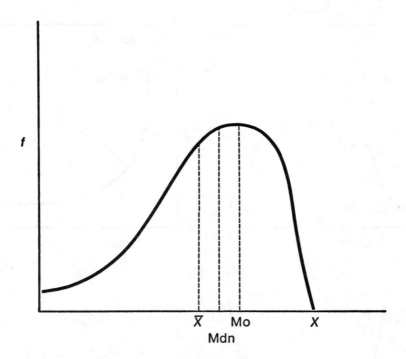

FIGURE 4.5. Negatively skewed distribution

more exact than eyeballing a graph, but it is beyond the scope of this book. Most computerized statistical-procedure packages, such as SPSSX, use the equation and measure the precise degree of skewness.

A less accurate but usually adequate way to determine skewness is to compare the values of the mean, median, and mode, but especially the mean and median. Observe in Figure 4.4 that the mean is numerically greater than the median. This means that there is some degree of positive skewness. In Figure 4.5 the mean is numerically less than the median. This, then, implies some degree of negative skewness. The size of the difference between the

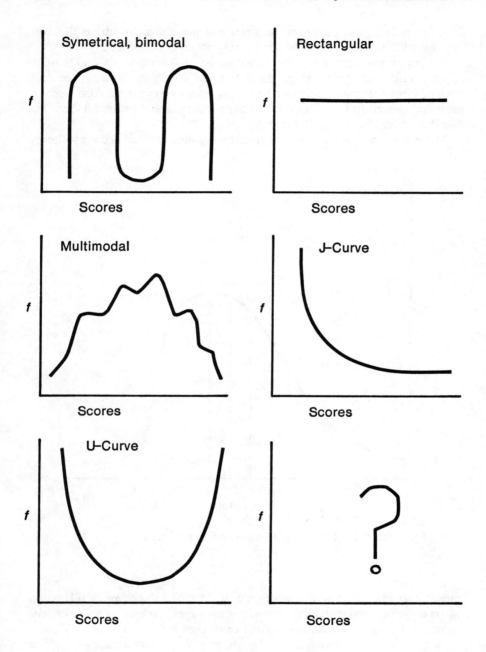

FIGURE 4.6. Other shapes of score distributions

median and the mean gives an indication of how much the distribution is skewed. In distributions of real data, it is the rule rather than the exception, that the mean and median will take on different values. Some of the differences are little, some are great. If a distribution is markedly skewed, we should use the median and not the mean to serve as our representative score. If the distribution is little to moderately skewed, we usually are on safe ground to use the mean. The problem we face is that there is no accepted definition or rule of thumb as to how great the difference must be before we decide a distribution is "markedly" skewed. In many cases, our safest course of action is to report both measures of central tendency. In other cases we may be able to rely on experience with the kinds of data we are working with to help us make this decision. To repeat ourselves, it is more desirable to be able to use the mean as our single representative score, since this would enable us to use a precise measure of the variability in a set of scores, as we will see later.

Distributions of real data do not always arrive in the form of unimodal configurations. Figure 4.6 shows some of the other shapes of score distributions we encounter, and the labels we attach to them.

Chapter 5

Measuring Variability

People vary. This astounding revelation is known by several cryptic terms, but it is most frequently referred to as Craft's Law of the Obvious. People are not the only things that vary. In fact, there are very few entities in the world that do not vary in one way or another. The variety around us is extremely important; without it life would indeed be bland.

Our job as social-service researchers (and, of course, as other kinds of researchers) in many ways boils down to trying to account for or to explain the variations we observe in clients, agencies, communities, etc. Why does one client benefit from treatment and not another? Why does one agency operate more efficiently than another? Why does child abuse occur more frequently in one community than another? These questions and the myriad of others we can ask all imply some degree of variation in what we are studying. The first question suggests that a measure of client outcome would show differences (variance) in client-outcome scores. The third question suggests that communities differ (vary) in incidence of child abuse.

Before we can begin to account for or explain the variations we observe, we must have a way to measure and describe this variance. The concept of *variance* of scores, or *dispersion* of scores, is very important. In fact, it may be *the* most important concept in the field of statistics.

We learned in Chapter 4 how to compute and interpret some central-value statistics that give us *one number* to represent all the numbers in a set of scores. However, a measure of central tendency is not sufficient to fully and properly describe a set of data. The reason is that such measures focus attention on only one aspect of the data, centrality, and in doing so suppress, or ignore, any information that shows the extent to which the data depart from centrality. We would like to have a single number that describes "spread," or "dispersion," around those scores that are of central value. There are several such statistics in common use. They are known as *measures of variability*. We will present and discuss three of these measures.

THE RANGE

The *range* is the most primitive of our measures of variability. The range is determined for a distribution by subtracting the lowest-score value from the highest-score value, or

$$R = \text{Highest} - \text{Lowest}$$

Suppose we had the following therapy outcome scores for clients under two different modes of therapy.

Therapy A	Therapy B
$\bar{X} = 32$	$\bar{X} = 32$
Mdn $= 32$	Mdn $= 32$
$Mo = 32$	$Mo = 32$
$N = 40$	$N = 40$

From what we learned in Chapter 4 about central tendency, what can we infer about the two sets of outcome scores? First, since the three measures are identical for both therapy groups, we know the distributions of $N = 40$ each are symmetrical about the midpoint. Second, we know that, *on the average*, the performance of the two groups was the same. Thus, we might be persuaded to infer that Therapy A and Therapy B produce very similar outcomes. But do they? Let's add one more piece of information from each data set. Let's assume that the range of scores for Therapy A is 10 and that for Therapy B is 20. Given that the distributions are symmetrical, we can further determine that the high score for A is approximately $\bar{X} + \frac{1}{2}R$ or $32 + 5 = 37$. The low score would be $32 - 5$, or 27. Thus, scores for Therapy A range from 27 to 37. If we use a similar procedure for Therapy B scores, we determine that scores range from 22 to 42. It appears that the scores for Therapy A are more closely bunched around their midpoint than are the Therapy B scores. This implies that, overall, Therapy A scores differ less from their mean and median than do Therapy B scores. Therefore, Therapy A scores are less variable than are Therapy B scores. But, are they really? If we base our thinking on the information presented, we cannot answer the question. It is possible that most of the Therapy B scores are clustered tightly around the midpoint, and the scores we use to compute the range are actually extreme, atypical scores. If this were true, then overall, Therapy B scores might be less variable. We could, of course, plot a histogram or polygon to solve this dilemma, but we don't want to have to do this each time we want to know how variable a set of scores are. We want a single measure that will reliably and accurately reflect score variability.

It should be clear that the range is a crude measure of variability. The use of the range as a measure of variability is, in some respects, like the use of the mode as a measure of central tendency. The mode, you will remember, is determined solely by the number of frequencies associated with a *single* score. The mode is totally insensitive to the rest of the score distribution. In a similar fashion, the range is determined exclusively by the two extreme scores. The range is not influenced by the position or magnitude of all the scores between these extremes. If either or both of these extreme scores happen to be unusually divergent, the range can imply too great a degree of dispersion, or scatter, among *all* of the scores.

Given these limitations of the range, we need a measure of variability that reflects how much *all* of the scores in a distribution deviate from each other.

THE AVERAGE DEVIATION

We could calculate how much each score in a distribution deviates from each and every other score in a distribution, and then find the mean of these deviations, or average deviation (AD). But to do this is an arduous task indeed. If we have 40 distinct score values in a distribution, this would require at least $(40 \times 39)/2$, or 780, deviations to be determined, then multiplied by their respective fs, summed, and the result divided by N. Not simple.

What we prefer is to have a measure that determines how much each score deviates from a *single* score in the distribution. If we are using the mean as our measure of centrality, then we can calculate how much each score deviates from the mean, and find the mean of these deviations. In other terms, we can compute

$$AD = \frac{\Sigma f(X - \bar{X})}{N}$$

But a problem arises because $\Sigma f(X - \bar{X}) = 0$ for any distribution of scores. In fact, calculating this sum is one way of verifying that one has calculated the mean correctly. The point here is that the algebraic sum of deviations from the mean is *always* zero, no matter how great N is.

To solve this problem, we sum the deviations without regard to the sign (minus or plus) of the deviation. Scores less in value than the mean produce negative (−) deviations; scores greater than the mean produce positive (+) deviations. When the sign of the numbers is ignored and the numbers are all treated as though they were positive, we are dealing with the *absolute values* of the numbers. The symbolic notation for absolute value is | |. When these two vertical bars flank a number, we treat the number as positive regardless of its sign. Thus $|9| = 9$ and $|-9| = 9$, so $-9 = 9$.

The average deviation from the mean must be computed from the *absolute values* of all deviations:

$$AD_x^- = \frac{\Sigma f|X - \bar{X}|}{N}$$

Table 5.1 shows the violence-shelter clients' ages used previously in Table 3.9. The second column (*B*) lists the frequencies for the ages. Columns *C*, *D*, and *E* illustrate the successive steps necessary to compute $AD\bar{X}$. In column *C*, the mean value of 27.82 years is subtracted from each age value. Note that this process results in a negative number for values of X less than 27.82. In column D, the f for each age is multiplied by the result in column C. Column E is the same as column D, except all negative signs are removed by taking the absolute values of the numbers in column D. Note that adding the numbers in column C results in a sum of zero. The $AD\overline{X}$ is computed by adding the numbers in column E, and then dividing the sum by N, or 44.

$$AD\overline{x} = \frac{\Sigma f |X - \overline{X}|}{N} = \frac{280.92}{44} = 6.38$$

For this distribution, we can state that "the average amount the age scores deviate from the mean age for the distribution is 6.38 years."

The average deviation has all the properties of any arithmetic average, and therefore for most data yields a very descriptive representation of "dispersion" among the scores.

It should be evident that as a set of scores scatter out more and more from the mean, the *absolute* values of the *deviations* associated with the scores will

TABLE 5.1. Average deviation of scores from mean and median for age of violence-shelter clients

(A) Age (X)	(B) f	(C) (X−X̄)	(D) f(X−X̄)	(E) f|X−X̄|	(F) (X−Mdn)	(G) f(X−Mdn)	(H) f|X−Mdn|
17	1	−10.82	−10.82	10.82	− 8.3	− 8.3	8.3
18	1	− 9.82	− 9.82	9.82	− 7.3	− 7.3	7.3
19	3	− 8.82	−26.46	26.46	− 6.3	−18.9	18.9
20	3	− 7.82	−23.46	23.46	− 5.3	−15.9	15.9
21	1	− 6.82	− 6.82	6.82	− 4.3	− 4.3	4.3
22	6	− 5.82	−34.92	34.92	− 3.3	−19.8	19.8
24	3	− 3.82	−11.46	11.46	− 1.3	− 3.9	3.9
25	5	− 2.82	−14.10	14.10	− 0.3	− 1.5	1.5
26	1	− 1.82	− 1.82	1.82	0.7	0.7	0.7
27	1	− 0.82	− 0.82	0.82	1.7	1.7	1.7
28	3	.18	0.54	0.54	8.1	8.1	8.1
29	4	1.18	4.72	4.72	3.7	14.8	14.8
30	1	2.18	2.18	2.18	4.7	4.7	4.7
32	2	4.18	8.36	8.36	6.7	13.4	13.4
33	1	5.18	5.18	5.18	7.7	7.7	7.7
34	2	6.18	12.36	12.36	8.7	17.4	17.4
35	2	7.18	14.36	14.36	9.7	19.4	19.4
39	1	11.18	11.18	11.18	13.7	13.7	13.7
49	2	21.18	42.36	42.36	23.7	47.4	47.4
67	1	39.18	39.18	39.18	41.7	41.7	41.7

$N=44$ $\Sigma=0$ $\Sigma=280.92$ $\Sigma=110.8$ $\Sigma=270.6$

Note: $\overline{X} = 27.82$ and Mdn $= 25.3$ for this distribution

get greater. Therefore, for a given size of N, the *average of those deviations will become greater*. It is essential to note that the magnitude of the original scores does not influence $AD\bar{X}$; the only important factor is how much the scores differ in value from the mean. If we added 5 years to every age score in Table 5.1, and recomputed $AD\bar{X}$, we would find that $AD\bar{X}$ would still equal 6.38. The dispersion of scores about the new mean (which would now be 32.82) would not be altered.

Although we usually think of average deviation from the mean, we can also compute the average (mean) absolute deviation from the median (Mdn), or any other point. To compute ADmdn, we must compute the absolute difference of each score from the median, sum, and divide by N. This is illustrated in columns F, G, and H of Table 5.1. The average deviation from the median is defined as

$$AD\text{mdn} = \frac{\Sigma f |X - \text{Mdn}|}{N}$$

So for the data in Table 5.1:

$$AD\text{mdn} = \frac{270.6}{44} = 6.15$$

We can say now that, disregarding sign, the average deviation of each age score from the median age is 6.15 years.

You may have observed in our examples that ADmdn is less than $AD\bar{X}$. This will always be true when a score distribution is skewed. If a distribution is not skewed, that is, if it is symmetric, the mean and median will be identical and $AD\bar{X}$ will equal ADmdn. This observation leads to the general rule mentioned in Chapter 4 that *whenever a distribution is markedly skewed, the median is the* preferred statistic to use as a measure of *central tendency* or as the basis for a measure of dispersion. This is so because the median is the point in a distribution which is closest (in terms of its absolute value) to all other scores in the distribution.

The average absolute deviation has two properties that make it a good index of variability:

1. As the dispersion of scores increases or decreases, $AD\bar{X}$ and ADmdn will become larger or smaller proportionately.
2. $AD\bar{X}$ and ADmdn are sensitive to the position of every score in a distribution, thus any change of any score influences the size of $AD\bar{X}$ and ADmdn.

It is readily apparent that any "good" measure of variability should have at least these two properties. If our only interest is doing *descriptive* statistics on data, then these two properties are enough. But, if we are interested in doing further statistical applications, the AD is, for all practical purposes, a dead-end statistic. Once computed, there is little more that can be done with it. There is, however, another measure of variability that has both properties necessary for statistical description, plus some other characteristics of importance primarily for the purpose of doing *inferential statistics* on data. This measure of variability is called the *standard deviation*. The standard deviation provides us with more information about the distribution than does the *AD*. Because of its broader utility in literature involving statistical description, the standard deviation is used almost exclusively as the index of variability.

THE STANDARD DEVIATION
Just as the average deviation is based on the concept of absolute deviations from some norm, the standard deviation is based on the concept of *squared deviations* from the mean.

Table 5.2 gives the squared deviations from the mean and median for the age scores we used in Table 5.1. Column 4 contains the squared deviations from the mean and column 6 contains the squared deviations from the median. Note that $f(X-\bar{X}^2)=3766.5$ is less than $f(X-Mdn)^2=4055.56$. This will always be so, unless $\bar{X}=Mdn$, for the mean is that point in a distribution that minimizes squared deviations (just as the median is that point that minimizes absolute deviations). This is sometimes called the *least squares*

TABLE 5.2. Squared deviations from the mean and median for age of violence-shelter clients

(1) Age (X)	(2) f	(3) $(X-\bar{X})^2$	(4) $f(X-\bar{X})^2$	(5) $(X-Mdn)^2$	(6)4 $f(X-Mdn)^2$
17	1	117.07	117.07	68.89	68.89
18	1	96.43	96.43	53.29	53.29
19	3	77.79	223.38	39.69	119.07
20	3	61.15	183.46	28.09	84.27
21	1	46.51	46.51	18.49	18.49
22	6	33.87	203.23	10.89	65.34
24	3	14.59	43.78	1.69	5.07
25	5	7.59	39.76	0.09	0.45
26	1	3.311	3.31	0.49	0.49
27	1	0.67	0.67	2.89	2.89
28	3	0.03	0.09	7.29	21.87
29	4	1.39	5.57	13.69	54.76
30	1	4.75	4.75	22.09	22.09
32	2	17.47	34.94	44.89	89.78
33	1	26.83	26.83	59.29	59.29
34	2	38.19	76.38	75.69	151.38
35	2	51.55	103.10	94.09	188.18
39	1	124.99	124.99	187.69	187.69
49	2	448.59	897.18	561.69	1123.38
67	1	1535.07	1535.07	1738.89	1738.89
			3766.50		4055.56

principle. Thus, when we use the mean to express central tendency, we use the standard deviation to express the variability in the data. When the median is used descriptively to express central tendency, it is often accompanied (or, if not, should be) by the average absolute deviation from the median to indicate dispersion.

A generic-standard deviation can be expressed by the letters SD. There are three different situations in which we use a SD to measure variability. We will use a different symbol to denote which of the three SDs we are working with. As we introduce and use these symbols, we hope you do not contract a case of neoiconophobia, an extreme and unreasonable fear of new symbols. One of the SDs calls for a modified formula for the *SD*. The three symbols and their respective situations are: σ, s, $\hat{\sigma}$.

σ (sigma) is a *parameter* of the population and is used to *describe* variability when we have all of the data from the population. Many times we cannot obtain measurements on the population of interest, and a sample is the best we can do (and is often quite adequate). A sample of scores is a subset of a population of scores. The population of scores itself may be a subset of an even larger body of scores, in which case it would then be considered a sample. Whether we call a set of scores a sample or population depends on what we intend to do with the data. We use the symbol s for the *SD* of a *sample*. We use s when we wish to describe variability in a sample. A *statistic* of a sample is called s. Very often we want to *infer* something about a population based on sample data. We then use $\hat{\sigma}$ when we want to *estimate* the population parameter σ. As you will see, the formula for $\hat{\sigma}$ is slightly different from the formulas for σ and s.

Both σ and s are used to describe the variability of some data on hand. The two are calculated with the same formula. We will describe two methods for calculating these *SD*s—the deviation-score method and the raw-score method. The two methods give the same answer. The deviation-score method gives a better understanding of what a *SD* is, but it is often more cumbersome to use if you are working with complex numbers. The raw-score method is more accurate, since it is not as susceptible to rounding errors.

DEVIATION METHOD

The formula used with this method is often referred to as the definitional formula for the SD, since the structure of the formula defines the *SD*.

The basic formula for computation of the SD as a descriptive index for *ungrouped* data is

$$\sigma = \sqrt{\frac{\Sigma (X - M)^2}{N}} \text{ or } s = \sqrt{\frac{\Sigma (X - \bar{X})^2}{N}}$$

Where σ = the SD of a population
μ = the mean of a population (pronounced "mew")
N = the number of deviations for either a population or a sample

     s = the SD of a sample
     $\bar{X}$ = the mean of a sample (pronounced "ex-bar")

As you can see, the formulas are the same except for the symbols denoting the means. Since they are the same structurally, and also because we often are not working with populations of scores, for the remainder of this discussion, we will concentrate only on s, the sample *SD*. (If the occasion should arise where one wants to calculate the *SD* for a population, the equation for s may be used and the numerical result denoted as σ).

As the formula indicates, the SD is a sort of average of the deviations from the mean; thus, the SD is often interpreted as the average amount that scores deviate from the mean. It is sometimes called a root-mean-square because it is the square root of the mean of the squared-deviation scores.

To calculate s, you must first calculate the mean, $\bar{X}$. Next you subtract the mean from each of the N scores, square each of these deviations, and add the squared deviations. This much of the process is symbolized by the portion of the formula $\Sigma(X-\bar{X})^2$. This term is called the *sum of squares* and is abbreviated *SS*. We next divide $\Sigma(X-\bar{X})^2$, or *SS*, by N. The result of this operation is called the *variance*, or *mean square*. The variance, or mean square, is a very important concept in the use of inferential statistics. We will merely note here that in the process of calculating *SD*, the variance is also computed. Our final step is to take the square root of $\Sigma(X-\bar{X})^2/N$, or *SS*/N, or the variance. The result is the *SD* for our sample. Thus,

$$s = \sqrt{\frac{\Sigma(X-\bar{X})^2}{N}} = \sqrt{\frac{SS}{N}} = \sqrt{\text{Variance}}$$

When working with actual data, we usually have our data organized into a frequency distribution, or grouped data. This necessitates a small modification of our SD formula to account for the f for each possible score value. This is the same consideration we had when computing $\bar{X}$ from grouped data. The SD formula for grouped data is

$$s = \sqrt{\frac{\Sigma f(X-\bar{X})^2}{N}}$$

You begin the calculation by computing $\bar{X}$. The remainder of the process is illustrated in Table 5.2. You next subtract the mean from each score value and square the difference (column 3). Then multiply each squared difference by its respective f, and sum these products. The result is $\Sigma f(X-\bar{X})^2$ or SS. After dividing SS by Σf or N, the square root of SS/n is s. Using the data in Table 5.2,

$$s = \sqrt{\frac{\Sigma f(X-\bar{X})^2}{N}} = \sqrt{\frac{3766.5}{44}} = \sqrt{85.60} = 9.25$$

We can now say that the mean age of shelter clients in this study is 27.82 years, and that the standard deviation of these ages is 9.25 years. Since this distribution is markedly skewed, both the mean and *SD* are greatly influenced by the two extreme age scores of 49 and 67.

The deviation method for calculating s is useful when N is large and no calculation aids are available. The deviation method keeps numbers smaller and thus more manageable. When a computer is not available, but a calculator is, and when both N and the size of the scores are small, the raw-score method is usually more convenient than the deviation method. And since we usually round off with the deviation method and we don't with the raw-score method, the raw-score method is more exact.

Two formulas are widely used for calculating s from raw data. Both formulas will be illustrated by using the data in Table 5.3. The data in Table 5.3 are self-esteem scores for 26 clients who are undergoing treatment at a mental-health center for a condition labeled bulimia. These are scores from

TABLE 5.3. Self-esteem scores for 26 bulimic clients and the SD for these scores

X	f	fX	X²	fX²
17	3	51	289	867
19	1	19	361	361
21	3	63	441	1323
24	2	48	576	1152
25	3	75	625	1875
26	2	52	676	1352
27	2	54	729	1458
28	4	112	784	3136
31	2	62	961	1922
32	1	32	1024	1024
33	1	33	1089	1089
34	1	34	1156	1156
36	1	36	1296	1296
$N=26$		$\Sigma fX=671$		$\Sigma fX=18{,}011$

$$\bar{X} = \frac{\Sigma fX}{N} = \frac{671}{26} = 25.808$$

$$S = \sqrt{\frac{\Sigma fX^2}{N} - \bar{X}^2} = \sqrt{\frac{18011}{26} - (25.808)^2} = \sqrt{692.73 - 666.05}$$

$$= \sqrt{26.68} = 5.165$$

or,

$$S = \sqrt{\frac{\Sigma fX^2 - \frac{(\Sigma fX)^2}{N}}{N}} = \sqrt{\frac{18011 - \frac{(671)^2}{26}}{26}} = \sqrt{\frac{18011 - 17316.96}{26}}$$

$$= \sqrt{26.69} = 5.166$$

testing prior to treatment, and the higher the score, the lower a client's self-esteem. Since we usually do our computations from a frequency distribution, only those formulas for such grouped data are presented. The first formula is

$$s = \sqrt{\frac{\Sigma f X^2}{N} - \bar{X}^2}$$

where $\Sigma f X^2$ = sum of the frequencies times the squared scores, and $\bar{X}^2$ = the sample mean squared. To apply this formula, the mean is first calculated $\bar{X} = \Sigma f X / N$. The next step requires a word of caution. To obtain $f X^2$ values, multiply each $f X$ value by X. *Do not square the* fX *values. To do so would result in the value* $f^2 X^2$, *which is not called for by the formula.* You could square each X and then multiply each X^2 by its frequency to obtain $f X^2$; however, it is simpler (according to the Law of Least Effort) to multiply $f X$ (which you already have from calculating $\bar{X}$) by X to obtain $f X^2$. After summing the $f X^2$ column divide $\Sigma f X^2$ by N and subtract the squared mean. This difference *must be* a positive number. Extract the square root to obtain s.

The other computational formula, that does not require the calculation of the mean, is

$$s = \sqrt{\frac{\Sigma f X^2 - \frac{(\Sigma f X)^2}{N}}{N}}$$

where all terms are defined as before. Users of this formula sometimes become confused over the difference between the terms $\Sigma f X^2$ and $(\Sigma f X)^2$. Be sure you understand the difference. The term $\Sigma f X^2$ is obtained by multiplying each $f X$ by X to obtain $f X^2$ and then summing the $f X^2$ column. The term $(\Sigma f X)^2$ is obtained by summing each $f X$ and then squaring $\Sigma f X$.

Table 5.3 shows the results of applying these two computational, or raw score, formulas for s to the sample of self-esteem scores. Note that there is a slight difference in the magnitude of s (5.165 vs. 5.166). Primarily this difference was produced by rounding off the squared mean.

We indicated earlier that we often use sample values (statistics) to estimate population values (parameters). Assume we take a large number of samples from a given population of scores and calculate $\bar{X}$ and s for *each* sample. The sample mean ($\bar{X}$) is called an *unbiased* estimator of the population mean (μ) because a sample mean does not tend to underestimate or overestimate the actual value of the population mean. If we averaged the sample $\bar{X}$s, we would find that the mean of the $\bar{X}$s is μ, the population mean. However, if we average the sample s's, we would obtain a value *less than* the value of the population SD, or σ. Thus, we call s a *biased* estimate for σ. To compensate for this error in estimation, we have to adjust the sample SD in such a manner that we get an unbiased estimate for σ from sample data. It turns out that the following produces the desired result:

$$\hat{\sigma} = \sqrt{\frac{\Sigma(X - \bar{X})^2}{N-1}}$$

If we divide by $N-1$ instead of N (as we did for s), we increase the value of the SD. Observe that for small samples, there could be a large discrepancy between s and $\hat{\sigma}$. For larger samples the difference between the two SDs becomes negligible.

INTERPRETING THE AD AND SD

As a descriptive measure, the standard deviation provides an index of how much scores in a distribution differ from each other and, in particular, from the mean. But when do we have a "little" variability? When do we have a "lot of" variability? There are no absolute standards on which to form an answer to these questions when we are considering a single-score distribution. The usefulness of these descriptive measures emerges when we start to compare distributions of scores. For example, our child-abuse age data (Table 3.6) produce an $\bar{X} = 6.947$ years and $s=4.915$. Interpretation of the mean is straightforward; the value of 6.947 is the "balance" point for these 6,669 ages. But what of the $s=4.915$ years? Other than loosely referring to this as "the average deviation of the ages is about 4.9 years," the utility is limited unless we compare this s to the s from a different-score distribution. Let us do just that. In Table 4.1 we observed a score distribution of ages at first placement into foster care for 386 children. The range for these data is 17 years, very similar to the 18 years for child-abuse ages. The mean age at first placement is $\bar{X} = 11.907$ years, and the $s=4.304$ years. When we compare these two age distributions, we can conclude that, on the average, children are placed into foster care at a much older age than the age we observed for reported child-abuse victims. In addition, the foster-care ages are less dispersed across the age range than are child-abuse ages. In other words, children going into foster care are more similar to each other in age than are children reported as victims of abuse. We can visualize this difference in variations by inspecting Figures 3.4 and 3.5. The distribution in Figure 3.5 is flatter, or more "spread," than that in Figure 3.4.

For these kinds of interval-scaled data, we could use, compare, and interpret average deviations in a manner similar to what we do with standard deviations. It is possible to use the AD and SD as descriptive and comparative measures on ordinal data, but we must exercise caution in how we interpret the values we obtain. The more confident we are that our ordinal scales approximate interval scales, the more assured we become in attaching any meaning to these measures.

INDEX OF DISPERSION (D)

What do we do if we have nominal data or data that are clearly no more than ordinal? How do we describe the variation these kinds of data possess? The concept of variation in scores is not limited to interval-level data. One measure of dispersion that we can apply to nominal and ordinal data is called the index of dispersion (D).

The index of dispersion is a ratio whose numerator and denominator are counts of numbers of pairs of scores. Assume a variable has k categories. The denominator of the ratio is the maximum number of unique pairs that can be created out of the scores such that each member of the pair is different. It turns out that this condition is met when the N scores or cases are evenly distributed among the k categories into which the scores are grouped. This is a situation where we would have maximum variability in a nominal, or ordinal, variable.

We will use some data from our domestic-violence shelter study to illustrate the logic. The following shows how the variable "ethnicity" was distributed in this study. Here $N=45$ and $k=3$:

Ethnicity	f
Black	2
White	40
Other	3
	$N=45$

If variability among the 45 scores were a maximum, there would be 15 scores in each of the 3 categories. The number of pairs of cases where the members of a pair come from *different* categories would be 675. That is, 15 pairs could be formed by pairing each of the black people with each of the white people. Since there are 15 black people, this would give $15 \times 15 = 225$ pairs. The same pairing would occur between black and "other," and between white and other, yielding a total of $225 + 225 + 225 = 675$ pairs. But, in this example the cases are not evenly distributed over categories; they are more concentrated than that. If we pair the 40 whites with the 2 blacks, we get 80 pairs. The pairing of whites with "other" produces 120 pairs (40×3), and the last pairings net 6 pairs (2×3). Thus, the total number of unique pairings for this distribution is $80 + 120 + 6 = 206$. The D statistic is simply a ratio of the number of different pairs that could be made out of the data at hand, compared with the maximum number of unique pairings that could be created if cases were evenly spread out over all *available* categories. Here $D = 206/675 = 0.305$.

If all scores were in a single category of a variable that has several possible categories, then there is maximum concentration of cases or minimum variability, and D would equal zero. On the other hand, if cases were evenly distributed among the possible categories, there would be maximum variability, and the numerator and denominator of the D ratio would be the same, and D would equal one (1). D varies then from zero to one and is a useful measure of variation for nominal or ordinal variables.

Let us look at another example to see how we might compare the variability of two nominal scaled, dichotomous variables. The variables chosen are from our foster-care study and are the gender of the foster children and the types of placement into foster care. The distribution for these variables are:

Gender	f	Placement	f
Male	279	Court Ordered	339
Female	133	Voluntary	72
$N=412$		$N=411$	

The computational formula for D is

$$D = \frac{k(N^2 - \Sigma f^2)}{N^2(k-1)}$$

where N is the number of scores; k is the number of categories of the variables (apart from whether all categories are used or not); f is the frequency for each category; and Σf^2 is the summation of the squared frequencies over the categories.

If you apply this formula to the gender variable, the result is

$$D = \frac{2(169,744 - 95530)}{169,744(2-1)} = \frac{148,428}{169,744} = 0.87$$

If you apply this formula to the type of placement data,

$$D = \frac{2(168,921 - 120,105)}{168,921(2-1)} = \frac{97632}{168,921} = 0.58$$

Remember now, the lesser the value of D, the less the variability, and the more the scores are concentrated. We can conclude, then, that our gender data are more variable ($D=.85$) than are the placement data ($D=.58$). This is to say that gender data are more evenly spread out over the gender categories than is true for the placement data.

SELECTING A MEASURE OF VARIABILITY

Several criteria might enter into the selection of a measure of variability. One criterion is the level of measurement for a particular variable. A second criterion is the measure of central tendency that makes the most sense to use.

For interval-level scores the standard deviation is the preferred measure of variability. If a distribution is severely skewed so that the mean is thought not to give an appropriate indication of central tendency, then the median and average deviation from the median would be likely candidates as measures of centrality and variability, respectively.

The selection of a measure for ordinal data is more problematic. The index of dispersion, D, is not sensitive to the ordering of categories implied in ordinal variables; thus D loses some information. On the other hand, measures that rely on distances along the variable scale, such as the standard deviation and average deviation, imply information in data that are not defined in the scores. A recommended resolution is to use the median for central tendency and the average deviation from the median for variation of ordinal data, while recognizing any potential over-interpretation of the latter.

For nominal, and perhaps ordinal variables, the index of dispersion provides us with a measure of variation in scores. D has a major advantage over the other measures of variation in that D varies on a scale from zero (for no variation) to 1.0 (maximum variation possible for data in hand). For the other measures the maximum possible magnitude of variation depends on the size of the score units used as well as the spread of the scores. Zero may indicate no variation for the range, average deviation, and the standard deviation, but beyond that the number obtained has little meaning in an absolute sense.

Z-SCORES

We have looked at measures of central value and measures of variability that can be used to describe distributions of scores. We now turn to a statistic, Z, which is used to describe a *single score* in a distribution.

A Z-score is a mathematical way to relate a raw score to the mean and standard deviation of its distribution.

$$Z = \frac{X - \bar{X}}{s}$$

Any distribution of raw scores can be converted to a distribution of Z scores. For each raw score there is a Z score. Raw scores that are above the mean will have positive Z scores; those scores that are below the mean will have negative Z scores. A Z-score is also called a *standard* score because it is a deviation score expressed in standard-deviation units. A Z distribution itself will have a mean equal to zero and a standard deviation equal to one. This is true no matter what the original X distribution.

What a Z describes is the relation of an X to its $\bar{X}$ with respect to the general width (variability) of the distribution. For example, we can say that a distance of 3 age units (or any score units) from X to $\bar{X}$ ($X - \bar{X} = 3$) is large or small only if we know how wide the entire distribution is. If a symmetrical distribution is 20 units wide and $\bar{X} = 30$, then $X = 40$ is the largest score. If the distribution is 40 units wide, then $X = 40$ is closer to the mean when compared to all other scores. What this means is that raw scores from different distributions cannot be compared unless the means and standard deviations are equal.

As an illustration, we will once again use the age distributions shown in Tables 3.1 and 4.1. Consider an age score of 9.5 years. For the child-abuse ages, this age is *greater* than the mean and has a Z-score of

$$Z = \frac{X - \bar{X}}{s} = \frac{9.5 - 6.947}{4.915} = \frac{2.553}{4.915} = 0.519$$

So in this distribution an age score of 9.5 years falls .519 standard deviations *above* the distribution mean. For the foster-care placement ages this age is *less* than the mean age and now has a standard score of

$$Z = \frac{X - \bar{X}}{s} = \frac{9.5 - 11.907}{4.304} = \frac{-2.407}{4.304} = -0.559$$

In this distribution an age score of 9.5 years falls 0.559 standard deviations below the distribution mean.

The use of the Z statistic permits us to assess the relative standing of a score in a distribution. The relative standing, as we have just seen, depends on the relationship of the score to the mean and the degree of variability in the distribution. We can also compare Z scores across distributions even when the distributions are measuring different things.

Another important use for the Z statistic is to express the percent of scores that fall within a specified number of standard deviations from the mean. If we have a distribution that is unimodal and symmetrical, the *minimum* percent of scores between $(\bar{X} + Z)s$ and $(\bar{X} - Z)s$ is *at least* equal to

$$100 \left[1 - \left(\frac{4}{9} \right) \left(\frac{1}{2} \right)^2 \right]$$

Thus, for any unimodal, symmetrical distribution, at least 56% of the scores fall within plus or minus one standard deviation from the mean because

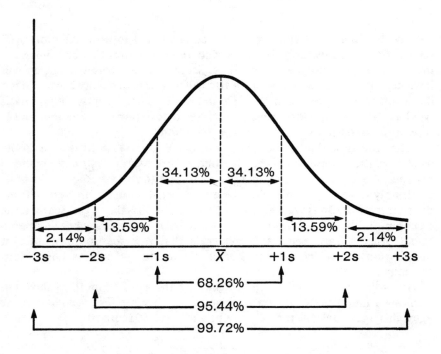

FIGURE 5.1. The normal curve and percent of scores within certain Z scores

$$\text{minimum percent} = 100 \left[1 - (\tfrac{4}{9})(\tfrac{1}{1})^2\right] = 100 \left[1 - \tfrac{4}{9}\right] = 56\%$$

Within two standard deviations from the mean, the minimum percent of scores is

$$100\left[1 - (\tfrac{4}{9})(\tfrac{1}{2})^2\right] = 100 \left[1 - (\tfrac{4}{9})(\tfrac{1}{4})\right] = 100 \,(\tfrac{8}{9}) = 89\%$$

The *minimum percent* of scores between the mean and plus and minus three-standard deviations is 95%; for plus and minus four-standard deviations it is 97%. A minimum of 99.6% of scores fall within plus and minus ten-standard deviations from the mean. Remember, when we talk of a score that is two- or three- or four-standard deviations from the mean, we are indicating a Z score of two or three or four.

If we know that a distribution is normal, then we may do an even more elegant description of our data. As we discussed in an earlier chapter, a normal distribution is unimodal, symmetric, and bell-shaped in form. Figure 5.1 shows that if a distribution is normal, then *precisely* 68.26% of the scores fall within Z scores of ± 1, or within plus or minus one standard deviation from the mean. *Exactly* 99.72% of the scores fall within Z-scores of ± 3.0.

There are prepared tables available that permit us to determine the exact percentage of scores that fall between any two points, or scores in a normal distribution. All that is required is to convert the raw X-scores to Z scores, and then enter the normal probability table at the proper points.

The normal curve or distribution is very important in the statistical treatment of data. If we know that a distribution is normal or at least approximates a normal curve, we are able to do a thorough job in a descriptive sense. The concept of the normal curve is especially important in the development and understanding of inferential statistics.

Chapter 6

Crosstabulation Analysis

So far in this book we have examined various statistics and procedures that describe a set of data. We have looked at ways to organize and present data and at measures that are used to indicate centrality and variability. We have found that there are certain procedures that can be applied to nominal data, and there are others that are applied to ordinal and interval data. But, in each case we applied these statistical techniques to one-variable distributions at a time. At this stage of our statistical growth, then, we are armed with a set of techniques that allows us to describe and present how the data for individual variables are distributed. Since these descriptive measures serve to describe individual variables, they are called univariate measures.

While many research questions and hypotheses involve single variables, even more consist of asking or stating something about the relationship or association between two or more variables. Is type of child abuse *related* to or *associated* with the age of the child? Another way to ask this is, "Is child abuse *dependent* on the age of the child?" We observed in our foster-care study that type of placement was predominantly court ordered. Is this true for both males and females? And if it is, is it to the same degree? Are women who are welfare recipients more likely to stay longer with an abusing spouse than women who are not welfare recipients?

Answers to questions such as these require that we go a step beyond the construction of individual-frequency distributions and look to see how our variables are jointly distributed. Rather than count how many clients are married or not and then counting how many are male or female, we can count how many males are married, how many females are married, how many males are not married, and finally, how many females are not married. A *joint-frequency distribution* of these counts would be entered into a table, such as Table 6.1, where a = the number of married males, b = the number of married females, and so on. This is called a 2 x 2 table (read "2 by 2" table).

The numbers $a + c$ and $b + d$ represent the number of males and females from an overall-frequency distribution for gender, and here they are called

TABLE 6.1. Example of a 2× 2 table

		Gender		
		Male	Female	
Marital status	Married	a	b	$a+b$
	Not married	c	d	$c+d$
		$a+c$	$b+d$	N

column totals. The numbers $a+b$ and $c+d$ are the number of married and not married from an overall-frequency distribution for the variable marital status and in this table are called row totals. If we sum the cell counts $(a+b+c+d)$, we obtain the total number (N) of cases distributed across the four cells. The row and column totals are also called marginal frequencies, since they are located in the margins of the table. It is the numbers within the cells that provide us with a joint distribution, and it is these numbers that concern us when we describe the relationship, or association, between variables.

There are several techniques available to present and measure the association between two or more variables. We will concern ourselves with those that seem to be most relevant to the kinds of data generated through social work research.

A bivariate *correlational analysis* provides us with a measure of the degree to which two interval-scaled or two ordinal-scaled variables are related. We will present two procedures commonly used for this purpose in the next chapter.

In this chapter we will concern ourselves with an examination of how we determine whether nominal (and sometimes ordinal) variables comprising a joint-frequency distribution are associated or not. To say that two variables are related, or associated, or dependent on each other, is to say that the distribution of values for one of the variables differs for different values of the other variable. If we find in a study that marital status is associated with gender, then we can say the proportions of married and non-married males differ from those of females.

We begin our procedure for generating joint-frequency distributions by doing what is called a cross-tabulation procedure, a cross-classification procedure, or a cross-break procedure. We will use the more familiar of the terms, crosstabulation, and shorten it to *crosstab*.

TABLE 6.2. Residential status by service receipt: version I

	Services		
	Yes	No	Row totals
Ruralites	O = 30 Rp = 60% Cp = 50% Tp = 30%	O = 20 Rp = 40% Cp = 50% Tp = 20%	50
Urbanites	O = 30 Rp = 60% Cp = 50% Tp = 30%	O = 20 Rp = 40% Cp = 50% Tp = 20%	50
Column totals	60	40	N=100

Before we look at some crosstabs generated from real data, we will use some hypothetical data to illustrate some of the variety of ways in which a crosstab can turn out. Keep in mind that when we are working with crosstabs, we are looking to see if the distribution of one variable depends on or is related to the distribution of another variable.

For convenience sake suppose we had data that indicated whether or not 50 rural residents and 50 urban residents had received services from a mental-health center. A crosstab for these two variables requires a table with rows (horizontal) and columns (vertical). The categories of one variable are labels for the rows, and the categories of the other variable are labels for the columns. Which variable do we place where? If one of the variables is construed to be the "dependent" variable, it will be used here as the column variable. The independent variable is then used as the row variable. The author has found after examining hundreds of crosstabs that this manner of setting up a crosstab facilitates the reading and interpretation of the table. However, it should be pointed out that others prefer the reverse location of the dependent and independent variables. Of course, if neither variable is thought to be more "dependent" than the other, then the variable placement is arbitrary. For our example, then, we have used resident status to define the rows and service receipt to define the columns. The question we are asking then is, "Does receipt of mental-health services *depend* on one's residential status?" These frequency data *could be* jointly distributed as presented in Table 6.2.

Let us first look at some of the table nomenclature. The "O" (oh) in each

**TABLE 6.3. Residential status by service receipt:
version II**

	Services		
	Yes	No	Row totals
Ruralites	O = 20 40%	O = 30 60%	50
Urbanites	O = 40 80%	O = 10 20%	50
Column totals	60	40	N=100

cell of the table stands for the "observed" frequency or count for that cell. When we look at the top, left cell, we see that 30 ruralites received services. Rp stands for "row percent," and indicates what percent in the cell O is of the total row count. In this case, the count of 30 is 60% of 50 (row total). "Column percent" is represented by Cp and indicates what percent the cell O is of the total column count. We find that 30 is 50% of 60. Finally, Tp stands for "total percent," which is the cell O divided by N, multiplied by 100. So 30% of the total N were ruralites who received services. It would be useful for you to work through these counts and percents for at least one other cell in Table 6.2.

If we look at the column totals, we see that 60% of 100 residents received services and 40% did not. For rural residents 30 of 50 (60%) received services, and the same was true for urban residents. Whether or not someone is an urban or rural resident has, according to these data, absolutely no bearing on whether or not they receive services. Another way of saying this is that whether or not one receives services is *independent* of residential status. So the knowledge that someone had received services would not help us at all in predicting or guessing the person's residential status. Or, in the reverse manner, the knowledge of someone's residential status helps us not a smidgen in determining whether or not that person has received services.

Now let us change the cell frequencies while maintaining *the same* marginal frequencies, and use only the row percents. This change is presented in Table 6.3.

Overall, we still have 60% of the residents receiving services. But, now we see that 80% of the urban and only 40% of the rural residents receive services. This is a rather large difference in the proportion of those receiving services. Thus, the pattern of row percentages for rural residents (40% and 60%) differ markedly from the row percentages for urban residents (80% and 20%). From a descriptive point of view with this data pattern, we are safe in concluding

TABLE 6.4. Residential status by service receipt: version III

	Services		
	Yes	No	Row totals
Ruralites	O = 29 58%	O = 21 42%	50
Urbanites	O = 31 62%	O = 19 38%	50
Column totals	60	40	N=100

that whether or not a person receives services is strongly *dependent* on whether that person is a rural or an urban resident. An urban resident is much more likely to be receiving services than is a rural resident.

Another way these two variables could be jointly distributed while keeping the same marginal frequencies is illustrated in Table 6.4. We now have a situation where the observed frequencies in each of the two rows are very similar in pattern. Sixty-two percent of the urbanites received services and 58% of the ruralites received services. Does receipt of services depend on residential status in this configuration of data? The answer is "yes," but it is a weak "yes." Urbanites are slightly more likely than ruralites to be service recipients. Is it possible that this type of finding would occur by chance alone? Quite likely. But for purposes of description, these two variables *are* related to each other in this particular case, even if it is ever so slightly.

Whenever we do a crosstab and observe that the *sets of row percentages are not* equivalent, the two variables in the table share *some* dependency on each other. Of course the same conclusion is reached when we compare sets of column percentages and find that they are not equivalent.

When we work with real data, we rarely observe complete independence of two variables in a cross-tab table. This means that we will usually find in our research data that two variables are related or associated. The important questions are, "To what *degree* are the variables in our sample data related? Is the association strong enough so that we can say we have a stable or reliable finding, or is the association so weak that we can attribute the row or column percent differences to chance fluctuations?" If our observed association is strong enough, and if we repeated our study, the odds are good we would once again find a similar association between the two variables. If our observed association in our sample is weak, then it is likely that in redoing the study we would find a different association, or none at all.

What we need here is some way to measure the strength of an association between two variables, and then we need some measure of the stability of our observed association.

PERCENTAGE DIFFERENCE

One measure of the strength of an association between two variables is the *percentage difference.* The basic rule for computing percentages on a table is to compute percentages in the direction of the independent variable. If we set up our crosstab as recommended, we have categories of the dependent variable across the top of the table (the head) and categories of the independent variable down the side (the stub). This is the way we set up Tables 6.2–6.4. With a table set up in this manner, we use the *row totals* as the base for percentages. Once the row percentages are computed for each row, we then contrast the distribution of the dependent variable between each of the categories of the independent variable. In our previous example we contrasted the distribution of receipt of services for each of the two residential statuses, rural and urban.

Comparisons are made in a table by examining differences between percentages. In Table 6.3, for example, we found a difference in percent for receipt of services of 40% (80% – 40% = 40%) among urbanites and ruralites. This value is called *epsilon,* the percentage difference in a crosstab. For tables that are larger than a two by two (2 x 2), there are a number of percentage contrasts that may be computed and used in interpretations.

If it is not clear which variable is dependent or independent, we can compute both *row and column percents* and examine the relationship in either or both direction(s). In Tables 6.3 and 6.4 we computed row percents, and this allowed us to examine any influence residence status may have on the distribution of receipt of service. However, in this example, examination of the relationship between the variables by computing and comparing column percents would not make much sense, since you would be asking if receipt of services in a mental-health center influences whether people live in urban or rural communities.

Epsilon can be used to determine if an association *exists at all* in a table of observed frequencies. We do this by computing percentages in one direction and comparing down in the other direction. That is, we compute row percentages and then compare row percentages in the columns. If all the epsilons that can be computed in a table amount to zero, then there is no association between the two variables crosstabulated into the bivariate distribution. This is called *statistical independence.* If, on the other hand, there is any epsilon that is not zero, then to that extent there is an association in the observed frequency table, however little or great that association may be. But just what does the size of epsilon tell us about the strength of an association between two variables?

The interpretation of epsilon depends not only on the pattern of frequencies within the table, but also on how balanced the marginal frequencies are

TABLE 6.5. Illustration of the use of epsilon as a measure of association

Illustration 1		

	Original table	Strongest possible association

	Services	Services

Ruralites	20	30	50	10	40	50
Urbanites	40	10	50	50	0	50
	60	40		60	40	
	Epsilon = 40%			Epsilon = 80%		

Illustration 2		

	Original table	Strongest possible association

	Services	Services

Ruralites	25	25	50	20	30	50
Urbanites	45	5	50	50	0	50
	70	30		70	30	
	Epsilon = 40%			Epsilon = 60%		

(row and column totals). To illustrate these constraints, consider the distributions in Table 6.5.

Illustration 1 of Table 6.5 shows the crosstab we saw in Table 6.3. We found that epsilon = 40% for these data. Given these marginal frequencies (row and column totals), how large can epsilon be? The maximum epsilon is determined by converting the smallest cell frequency to zero, adjusting the remaining cell frequencies, and recomputing cell percentages. The second table shows the pattern of frequencies for the strongest possible association. The epsilon for this table is 80% (100% - 20%). In the second illustration it is not possible, given the fixed marginals, to adjust cell frequencies to achieve an epsilon of 80%. The strongest possible association we can get with these marginals is 60%. Epsilon can equal 100% *only* when the marginal frequencies are balanced. In the first case then we have to interpret our epsilon = 40% in terms of a maximum possible of 80%. In the second case we also have an obtained epsilon of 40%, but this epsilon must be interpreted with respect to maximum possible of 60%. It is not appropriate to compare *directly* the two obtained epsilons because they reflect not only the pattern of frequencies in a table, but they are also constrained by the way the marginal frequencies are distributed. At this point, all we can say is that epsilon indicates that there is an association in both original tables. One solution to this comparison problem is to determine the ratio of an obtained epsilon to the maximum possible epsilon. Let's call this ratio the Craft Coefficient, or *CC*. In our first case here we would divide 40% by 80% to obtain a *CC* of 0.5. In the second case $CC = 0.67$ $(40/60 = .67)$. Now we can compare the two original tables and conclude that the second epsilon of 40% indicates a stronger association than the epsilon of 40% for the first table. The use of this derived measure *CC* permits us to compare strength of association in two 2×2 tables. To use this measure of association, then, we must (1) crosstabulate two, two-category variables, (2) compute epsilon, (3) compute the maximum epsilon, and (4) obtain *CC*. The derived measure *CC* can vary from 0 to 1.00; these values range from no association to maximum association possible.

Percent difference is often construed as a rough, or crude, measure of association. At a minimum the use of epsilon helps to determine if an association exists. Since *CC* is not a normed or standardized index of association at this time, the use of *CC* perhaps should be limited to comparisons of associative strength with respect to the *amount of association possible* in a given crosstab.

THE CHI-SQUARE

We can also check for the existence of an association in a crosstab by comparing the *actual observed table frequencies* with the frequencies we would expect if there were *no association,* or *expected frequencies.* If the match between actual, or observed frequency, data and expected-frequency data is perfect, then there is no association in the observed data between the two variables we have crosstabulated.

In setting up a model of the way frequencies should look in a table, if *there were no association,* we assume that the row and column totals (marginal distributions) are the same as in the observed-data table, and that the total number of cases is the same. The problem is to specify the pattern of cell frequencies in a way that shows no association. As an example, let us once again consider the data in Table 6.3. We note that overall 60% of the cases received services (60 of 100). If there had been no association between receipt of services and residence status, then 60% of the ruralites (30 of 50) and 60% of the urbanites should have received services (30 of 50). That is, we would "expect" the same proportion of these two groups to have received services. We signify observed frequences as *O*s and expected frequencies as *E*s. Table 6.6 shows the observed and expected frequencies for the data in Table 6.3.

Expected cell frequencies (*E*s) can be computed for any cell by multiplying

**TABLE 6.6. Residential status by service receipt:
Expected frequencies**

		Services		
		Yes	No	Row totals
Residence	Ruralites	O = 20 E = 30	O = 30 E = 20	50
	Urbanites	O = 40 E = 30	O = 10 E = 20	50
	Column totals	60	40	N=100

the row total for that cell by the column total for that cell, and dividing by N.
The E for the top left cell is determined by the formula

$$Expected = \frac{(50)(60)}{100} = \frac{3000}{100} = 30$$

Given that one of the expected-cell frequencies is computed in a 2 x 2 table, the
rest can be determined by subtracting, since the Es, like the Os, must add up
across rows and down columns to equal the row and column totals.

Once we have Es computed, we can compare the O and E for each cell. If all
of the O minus E comparison results amount to zero, then there is *no
association* between the two variables crosstabulated. If any of these
comparisons are other than zero, then an association exists between the two
variables. The association may be slight or weak, or it may be large. Our task
now is to use this no-association model to see if we can construct an index that
will help us determine the strength of association.

We want to start by measuring the discrepancy between an observed set of
frequencies and an expected set of frequencies that serve as a model for
statistical independence or no association. This is done by calculating a
measure called *chi-square* (χ^2).

$$\chi^2 = \Sigma \left[\frac{(O-E)^2}{E} \right]$$

This formula requires, for each cell, that we subtract E from O, square the
difference, and divide by E. We then sum these chi-square components. We
square the difference between O and E to eliminate negative differences and
divide the squared difference by E to help take out any effects of different
numbers of cases in a category of the row or column variables. Also, this

division of the squared difference for each cell by E takes out the effect of having different distributions of row and column totals in different cross-tabulation tables.

If we apply the formula for chi-square to the Table 6.3 data, we find that

$$\chi^2 = \frac{(20-30)^2}{30} + \frac{(30-20)^2}{20} + \frac{(40-30)^2}{30} + \frac{(10-20)^2}{20}$$

$$= \frac{(-10)^2}{30} + \frac{(10)^2}{20} + \frac{(10)^2}{30} + \frac{(-10)^2}{20}$$

$$= \frac{200}{20} + \frac{200}{30} = 16.67$$

Chi-square *per se* is not useful as a measure of magnitude of association, since it is not a standardized measure. Chi-square is very useful in inferential statistics, however, as we will see in Chapter 8.

Chi-square is always a positive number, and it will equal zero if there is no association in a table. However, the upper limit on the value of χ^2 depends on N and the size of the table. In fact, the upper limit on χ^2 is equal to $N(k-1)$, where N equals the total N for the table and k is the number of rows or columns in a table, whichever is the lesser number. For our example, the upper limit on χ^2 is 100, or simply N. If we doubled the N and kept the cell percents the same, the upper limit on χ^2 would increase to 200. Thus, for descriptive purposes, χ^2 is useful to indicate that an association *exists*, but it is not directly useful as a measure of the *magnitude*, or *strength*, of association. But there are other measures derived from χ^2 that are useful, and we will present a few of them here.

MEASURES OF ASSOCIATION BASED ON CHI-SQUARE

If we have a 2 x 2 table, the *phi* statistic is a suitable measure of the strength of association. The *phi* coefficient is obtained by dividing the χ^2 by N, and then extracting the square root of χ^2/N.

$$phi = \sqrt{\frac{\chi^2}{N}}$$

Phi varies from 0 (statistical independence) to a maximum of +1.0 (perfect association) for any table where at least one of the variables has only two categories. Unlike the chi-square, *phi* is unaffected by sample size. *Phi* is very appropriate for measuring and comparing strength of association in 2 x 2 crosstabulations of nominal- and ordinal-scaled variables. Only the magnitude of an association is indicated by *phi* and not the particular nature of an association. How two variables are related usually requires a visual inspection of the pattern of cell frequencies. The *phi* calculated for our data in Table 6.3 is

$$phi=\sqrt{\frac{\chi^2}{N}}=\sqrt{\frac{16.67}{100}}=\sqrt{.1667}=.408$$

For "square" tables larger than 2 x 2 (e.g., 3 x 3, 5 x 5), for which *phi* is not appropriate, the *contingency coefficient (C)* may be used. The formula for *C* is

$$C=\sqrt{\frac{\chi^2}{\chi^2+N}}$$

For tables larger than 2 x 2 the maximum value of *phi* exceeds 1.0. The contingency coefficient, however, cannot exceed 1.0 in magnitude, no matter what the size of the table. In fact the upper limit of *C* is a value less than 1.0, and it depends on the size of the table. The upper limit for a 2 x 2 table is .707 and for a 5 x 5 table the maximum *C* is .894. The *C* calculated for Table 6.3 data is

$$C=\sqrt{\frac{16.67}{16.67+100}}=\sqrt{\frac{16.67}{116.67}}=\sqrt{.1429}=.378$$

The contingency coefficient should only be used for comparison of crosstabs having the same number of rows and columns.

For tables larger than 2 x 2 and which are not square, we can use a measure of association called *Cramer's V*. The formula for Cramer's V is:

$$V=\sqrt{\frac{\chi^2}{N\times m}}$$

where *m* is defined as the lesser of the two numbers, $(r-1)$ or $(c-1)$. (*Remember:* $r=$ the number of rows and $c=$ the number of columns.)

Cramer's V can always attain a value of 1.0 even if the table is not square. It, like the other measures, equals zero if there is no association. The Cramer's V calculated for Table 6.3 data is:

$$V=\sqrt{\frac{16.67}{100(1)}}=\sqrt{.1667}=.408$$

You may have already noted that $V=phi$ for 2 x 2 tables.

Of the measures of association considered so far, Cramer's V would be the preferred measure of association for bivariate distributions of nominal variables. It is what is termed properly normed. The number or distribution of cases in row or column totals does not influence its value, nor is it influenced by the number of categories of either variable.

It is useful here to point out a few considerations we take into account before we apply crosstabs to a set of data. The underlying theme of this chapter is that we use crosstabs as an analytic tool to help determine if and how variables are associated. What kinds of variables can be crosstabulated? Variables at any level of measurement and with any number of categories (within reason of course) *can be* crosstabbed. However, for interval variables there are other, more appropriate techniques for displaying and measuring association. Crosstabs are especially suited for nominal and ordinal variables, with a further restriction being that variables should not have a great number of categories, say more than 5 to 7. While a crosstab can be constructed to display the joint-frequency distribution among variables with many categories, consider the problem that arises in trying to interpret and then describe the relationship among the variables. As the number of cells in a crosstab increases, so does the difficulty in describing the nature of the data within the table.

To control table size, it is sometimes necessary to reduce the number of categories for one or both of the variables by grouping categories. We discussed how this was done in Chapter 3. Grouping should only be done if the grouping procedure makes sense. We need to be careful that combining cells does not distort the association between two variables by artificially increasing or decreasing it.

We are interested in relationships among *variables*. This means that we try to determine if the variance we observe for one variable is related to or can "account" for the observed variance in the other variance. It follows, then, that each of the two or more variables entered into a crosstab should possess at least a modest degree of dispersion among the categories. For example, suppose we found in a study that 55% of a group of clients were successful in therapy and 45% were not. When we try to account for this difference in outcome success, it would be of little use to crosstab the outcome variable with client gender, *if* a large proportion of the clients (e.g., 90%) were one gender or the other. However, if gender were more evenly split, then a crosstab of these variables *might* reveal an association.

Before applying crosstab analysis to a set of data, it is useful to construct frequency distributions for individual variables. Inspection of these distributions can help determine which, if any, variables need to be reduced in number of categories and which variables will not lend themselves to being cross-tabbed. Very often we have these frequency distributions in hand anyway as part of our descriptive analysis of our data set.

We have now discussed several measures of association that may be applied to data displayed in a crosstab table. We must be clear that the measures considered *indicate only* the existence and strength of an association. These measures do not allow us to specify the percent of variation in one variable explained by another, nor can they be interpreted as the portion of predictive errors that may be reduced by prior knowledge of one of the variables. There are other measures that incorporate these features, but they will not all be discussed here. Having a numerical measure of the strength of an association and the visual inspection of a crosstab will usually suffice for adequate description of a relationship between nominal variables. In the next chapter we will consider two measures of correlation for ordinal and interval variables. The reader who wishes a more in-depth treatment of association is referred to the texts listed in the reference section.

CROSSTABS IN ACTION

Now that we are familiar with the structure of a crosstab table and several measures of association, we will once again use real data to illustrate how these analytic techniques can actually be used.

Our first example is from the study of domestic-violence shelter clients. In this study clients were asked in one part of the questionnaire if they were welfare recipients and in another part if a weapon was used in the abusing incident. The question we can address with crosstabs is whether the use of a weapon *depends* on whether the client is a welfare recipient or not. The data for this crosstab are shown in Table 6.7.

The marginals of Table 6.7 indicate that a weapon was used in 40% of the cases and also that 47% of the women were welfare recipients. Are the two variables associated? The layout of the table shows that "weapon" is our dependent variable and "welfare" the independent variable. This means we will only use *row percents* to determine the existence and magnitude of an association.

Note in Table 6.7 that epsilon = 20.4% and Cramer's V = .207. Both of these statistics indicate that a weak to moderate association exists between "weapon" and "welfare" *for this sample of 57 clients.* What is the nature of the association? Table 6.7 reveals that for those who are not welfare recipients, there is an even chance (50-50) of a weapon being used during an abusing incident. For welfare recipients there is greater likelihood of a weapon not being used than being used (30-70). There are two important points to make here about this association and others we might observe. First, we have not established a causal connection between use of a weapon and welfare status. That is, not being a welfare recipient *does not cause* a weapon to be used. All we can deduce from our crosstabs and statistics is that these variables are related. Second, the crosstabs and related statistics do not directly tell us about the larger population from which this sample came. Once again, all we know for sure is that these two variables are associated to some degree *in our sample.* We will see in Chapter 8 how we can determine the likelihood that this association also exists in the larger population of shelter clients. But since our primary interest now is to *describe* relationships of *data in hand,* the technique we have used is sufficient.

Our second example illustrates what might be expected if we observe a very weak association between two variables. Table 6.8 depicts a crosstab of age of a child and sex of the child reported as a victim of abuse. These data were extracted from the same child-abuse registry data we introduced in Chapter 2. These particular variables should be familiar, as we looked at them separately in Chapters 3 and 4. We would like this crosstab to help us determine if age is dependent on gender. That is, does the age distribution differ for female- and male-child abuse victims? Note that the age variable has been condensed into three categories from the original nineteen. Age is considered the dependent variable and consequently defines the columns. Gender is our independent variable that defines the rows. Once again we will compare distributions of row percentages.

TABLE 6.7. Observed frequencies and percentages for weapon used by welfare status for 57 shelter clients

		Weapon Used		
		Yes	No	Row totals
Welfare status	Yes	O = 8 29.6%	O = 19 70.4%	27 47.4%
	No	O = 15 50%	O = 15 50%	30 52.6%
Column totals		23 40.4%	34 59.6%	N=57

Epsilon = 20.4%; maximum epsilon = 76.7%; V = .207

The greatest epsilon in Table 6.8 is 6.1%. Cramer's V equals .063. Both measures signify a *very weak* relationship between these variables for *this sample of 6,640 cases.* Inspection of Table 6.8 indicates that male ages are evenly spread out over the three categories, whereas female ages *tend* to favor the highest category. We must keep in mind that our conclusion that age is *weakly* related to gender is based on an age variable reduced to three categories. This grouping may have distorted any "true" relationship between

TABLE 6.8. Crosstab of age and gender of child-abuse victims for registry data

		Age			
		0–3 yr	4–8 yr	9–18 yr	Row totals
Gender	Female	990 30%	993 30.1%	1312 39.8%	3295 49.6%
	Male	1114 33.3%	1103 33%	1128 33.7%	3345 50.4%
Column totals		2104 31.7%	2096 31.6%	2440 36.7%	N=6640

TABLE 6.9. Crosstab of type of report and year of report for child-abuse registry data

		Type of report			
		Physical abuse	Sexual abuse	Neglect	Row totals
Year	1977	97 76.4%	7 5.5%	23 18.1%	127 2.0%
	1978	375 48.3%	38 4.9%	364 46.8%	777 12.5%
	1979	492 31.4%	87 5.6%	987 63.0%	1566 25.2%
	1980	532 27.8%	90 4.7%	1290 67.5%	1566 30.8%
	1981	430 23.5%	96 5.2%	1303 71.2%	1829 29.4%
	Column totals	1926 31.0%	318 5.1%	3967 63.9%	$N=6211$

age and gender, but we cannot tell this from Table 6.8. We would have to construct a 2 x 19 crosstab (38 cells) to determine what the actual relationship is for this sample. But remember, establishing that an association exists at all is one matter; interpreting the relationship is another. It is important to know that how we group data may influence our observed relationships and any conclusions we may make.

Table 6.9 provides an example of a 5 x 3 crosstab. The data are again from the child-abuse report registry and the crosstab is between the type of abuse reported and the year of the report. Of interest here is whether the type of report distribution has changed over the years 1977 to 1981.

When we look at the row totals, we see that a large proportion of reports were made during 1980 and 1981. But this central registry did not come into existence until the latter part of 1977. We also remind the reader that these data comprise an approximately 10% sample of all of the reports made during the indicated years. But our interest is not in the observed frequencies per se;

we are interested in the distribution of proportions or percentages over the years. Note in Table 6.9 that as we proceed through the years 1977 to 1981, the *proportion* of reports for physical abuse decreases markedly (from 76.4% to 23.5%). The proportion of reports of sexual abuse remains fairly constant (about 5%), and the proportion of reports for neglect increases dramatically (18.1% to 71.2%). Most of these shifts in types of report made can be attributed to administrative-rule changes and modifications of the legal code pertaining to abuse and neglect. Since the start of this reporting system, there have been changes in the makeup of mandated reporters (those required by law to report suspected child-abuse cases) as well as changes in the definitions of abuse and neglect. The greater proportion of neglect reports than physical-abuse reports does not *necessarily imply that neglect occurs more often than* physical abuse; all we know for sure is that for a given number of cases, neglect will constitute a higher proportion of those reports. However, this is not to say that these are not important data. Administrators and supervisors in protective services can use trend data like that in Table 6.9 to assist in allocation of resources and training of staff.

The calculation of epsilon for Table 6.9 would serve little purpose, since there are so many (30) epsilons that can be computed. Cramer's V for these data is 0.212, indicating a moderate to weak association. But this statistic is small because of the constancy of the proportion of sexual-abuse reports. If the physical abuse and neglect categories only are used, the measured association will increase substantially.

MULTI-WAY CROSSTABS

In Chapters 3–5 we examined some common techniques for describing single variables. So far in this chapter we have concerned ourselves with techniques used to analyze and describe the relationship between two (nominal) variables. One- and two-variable analyses are common and useful, but many research problems we work with are not univariate or even bivariate but multivariate in nature. In a multivariate situation we are interested in examining the inter-relationships among three or more variables. While we can use multivariate techniques on four or more variables, we will focus our discussion on the analysis of three variables. In its simplest form the analysis begins by noting a relationship between two variables. We then select a third variable, called a *control variable,* and examine the original two-variable relationship as it exists for each category of the control variable. In some instances, an originally strong relationship will weaken or disappear. In other instances, a relationship that originally seemed to be virtually nonexistent will emerge, or a strong relationship may be shown to exist for one category of the control variable but not for another. We will use data from another study to illustrate the outcome of a three-way crosstab.

The data are from a study of police-officers' attitudes and experiences related to domestic-disturbance cases (see Appendix A). Police officers in five

TABLE 6.10. Crosstabulation of need for shelter by perceived increase in abuse for 179 police officers

		Shelter needed		
		Yes	No	Row totals
Increase in abuse	Yes	108 93.1%	8 6.9%	116 64.8%
	No	47 74.6%	16 25.4%	63 35.2%
Column totals		155 86.6%	24 13.4%	N=179

cities in a midwestern state participated in the study by completing a mailed questionnaire. Table 6.10 shows a crosstab of responses to two questions in the survey. In one part of the survey instrument, respondents were asked if in their professional opinion, spouse abuse has increased in their area during the past 5 to 10 years. In another part of the survey, respondents were asked if they perceived a need for a spouse-abuse shelter in their area. The research question before us is whether the perceived need for a shelter depends on the officers' perception of an increase in spouse abuse. We can readily speculate that those who indicate an increase in abuse would be more likely to indicate a need for a shelter than those who do not indicate an increase in abuse. Overall, these officers were more likely to perceive an increase in abuse (64.8% vs. 35.2%, column percentages) and were strongly supportive of the need for a shelter (86.6% vs. 13.4%, row percentages). Epsilon for this table is equal to 18.5%, but the maximum epsilon possible is only 38.1%. If we interpreted the 18.5% as a weak association without looking at the maximum epsilon possible, we might conclude that a weak association exists when in fact a moderate relationship exists. Cramer's V for Table 6.10 is equal to 0.260. Thus, Table 6.10 depicts a *moderate* strength association or dependency between the two variables. These data indicate that those officers who perceive an increase in abuse are also more likely to perceive a need for a shelter. Now let us introduce a third variable into the analysis, that being the five cities in which these officers serve. Does the relationship observed in Table 6.10 hold for each of the five cities, or does the strength of the observed dependency itself depend on this third variable? For purposes of example, we will only consider the original relationship (Table 6.10) for two of the cities.

Table 6.11 presents the crosstab of increase in abuse by need for a shelter

TABLE 6.11. Crosstab of increase in abuse by need for shelter for cities A & B

	Shelter needed		
City A	Yes	No	Row totals
Epsilon = 43.1%			
Max. Epsilon = 53.3%	27	1	28
Cramer's V = 0.528% Yes	96.4%	3.6%	65.1%
Increase in abuse			
	8	7	15
No	53.3%	46.7%	34.9%
Column totals	35	8	N=43
	81.4%	18.6%	

	Shelter needed		
	Yes	No	Row totals
	45	5	50
Yes	90.0%	10%	62.5%
Increase in abuse			
City B	24	6	30
Epsilon = 10% No	80.0%	20.0%	37.5%
Max. Epsilon = 36.7%			
Cramer's V = .14			
Column totals	69	11	N=80
	86.3%	13.7%	

for two cities, one with 43 survey respondents and the other with 80 respondents.

In this *elaborated* table we see that for City A, the original relationship is greatly changed. We now observe an epsilon of 43.1% and a V of 0.528. Both of these statistics indicate a *strong* relationship between the two variables for City A. For City B we observe that the original relationship has been *reduced somewhat*. Epsilon for City B data is only 10% and V is 0.14. Thus we can surmise that the original, overall relationship is comprised of five different relationships, varying in associative strength. That is, in fact, the case here.

This process of *elaboration* involves the re-analysis of a two-variable relationship by the introduction of a third variable, a control variable. The original pattern of association is analyzed for some or all of the categories of the control variable. When do we use this elaboration procedure in our descriptive data analysis? In some instances in an a priori fashion, we let our research questions and hypotheses help dictate which two-variable relationships we subject to scrutiny with a control variable. In other instances we find it necessary to introduce control variables during the interpretative phase of our analysis, when we are trying to "account for" or "explain" an observed relationship.

Chapter 7

Correlational Methods

Crosstabulations as a technique for displaying the joint-frequency distributions for two variables is best suited for variables with few categories and/or of nominal measurement. Many of the variables of interest to social workers are of this nature. But many variables measured at the ordinal and interval levels of measurement are also important in our task of establishing and quantifying relationships we observe in the world around us.

In this chapter we will devote our attention almost exclusively to two statistical measures of association, the Pearson product-moment correlation coefficient, r, and the Spearman rank-order correlation coefficient, r_s. The former is an index of the degree of relationship between two interval-scaled variables, and the latter measure indicates the magnitude of relationship between two rank-ordered variables (ordinal). When working with nominal or ordinal data, there are several statistics, each of which is, in the proper circumstances, an appropriate measure of association. In this chapter we will consider only the oldest of the frequently used measures of ordinal association. When working with interval-level data, our choice of statistic problem is greatly minimized by the fact that the Pearson r is the nearly universal choice as the measure of association. The Pearson r is important also because it is the basis of many advanced statistical techniques, which will not be presented here.

THE PEARSON r

It is with the Pearson r that we run into the first technical use of the term *correlation*. Correlation is frequently misused as a more technically-sounding equivalent of *relationship*. Correlation, like our concept of association, involves both a relationship *and* the concept of *quantification* of the *strength or degree* of relationship.

To have a correlation, we must have two variables, with values on one variable (X) paired in some *logical* way with values on the second variable (Y).

TABLE 7.1. Length of time in minutes to complete two client intake interviews

| Interviewer | Interview | |
	First	Second
Jim	13	13
Jack	18	18
Jane	15	15
Joe	22	22
Jill	20	20
Jean	19	19

One logical way (and the most typical) to obtain pairs of scores is to measure both X and Y on each case in a sample of cases. For example, we could measure the weight and height of N individuals. The weight and height pairings could then be subjected to analysis to determine the correlation between the two variables.

The Pearson r can be defined as the measure of "the magnitude and direction of linear correlation between two variables." Magnitude of relationship is a concept we discussed in Chapter 6. The concepts of "direction" and "linear" with respect to relationships will be dealt with shortly.

Two variables may be positively correlated, be negatively correlated, or have no relationship to each other (zero correlation). A *positive correlation* is the name given to the situation in which relatively large values for one variable (X) are associated with relatively large values in the other (Y) and relatively little values of X are associated with relatively little values of Y. As an example, there is a positive correlation between height and weight in children—in general. The taller the child, the heavier—in general. There are exceptions, of course, but they only indicate that this particular correlation is not a perfect one.

A *negative correlation* is one in which relatively great values of X are associated with relatively little values of Y, and relatively little values of X are associated with relatively great values of Y. Among adults there is a negative correlation between age and muscular strength—in general. As adults get older, they generally get weaker. Again, the exceptions merely show that this correlation is not perfect.

A *zero correlation* means that there is no relationship between X and Y. Greater values of X are associated with both great *and* little values of Y. Similarly, lesser values of X are paired with both little *and* great values of Y.

The Pearson r varies in direction and magnitude from -1.00 to $+1.00$. When $r = -1.00$, we have a perfect negative correlation; when $r = +1.00$, the relationship is positive and perfect; when $r = 0$, we have observed the lack of any relationship. For any r, the sign ($+$ or $-$) denotes the direction of a relationship, and the numerical value signifies the magnitude of relationship.

DISPLAYING CORRELATION GRAPHICALLY

A graphical plot of the correlation between two variables is called a scatterplot or *scattergram.* A scattergram is constructed by placing one variable along the abscissa and the other along the ordinate. If one of the variables is considered to be the "independent" variable, this variable is placed along the abscissa. The next step involves constructing a distribution of *pairs* of *scores.* It is then that the values for each pair are plotted in the scattergram. Let's demonstrate this with a simple, hypothetical example. We remind you that nearly all of the procedures detailed in this book are usually carried out by a computer, even the plotting of a scattergram. But even though we rely on our friend, the machine, to do most of our labor, it is important to know the steps undertaken by our friend.

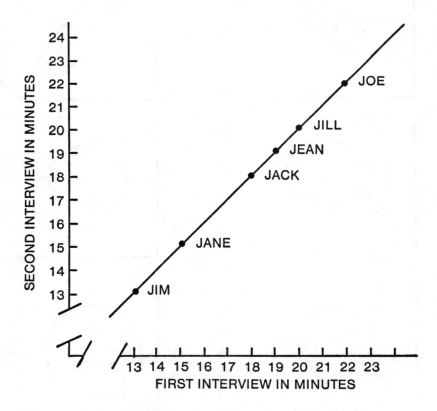

FIGURE 7.1. Length of time in minutes to complete two client intake interviews

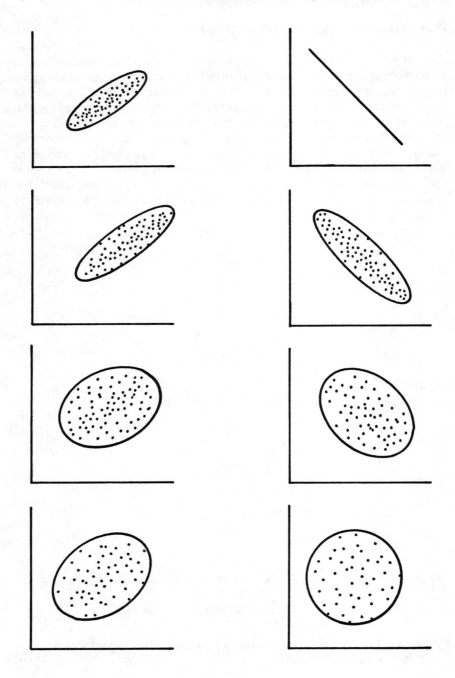

FIGURE 7.2. Idealized scattergrams formed by drawing envelope around points

Now, suppose we randomly select six social workers and measure the time it takes them to do each of two client-intake interviews. Table 7.1 shows how the data *might* come out. The first important thing to notice in Table 7.1 is that the interviewers' names all begin with "J." The second thing to note is that, for each worker, interview time is the same. It appears from Table 7.1 that the time it takes to do a second interview is highly associated with the time it takes to complete a first interview. In fact, it appears as if there might be a *perfect correlation* between the two variables. A graphical plot of this relationship would look like that shown in Figure 7.1.

Examine Figure 7.1 carefully. Each point represents a pair of scores—first-interview time and second-interview time. The line that runs through the points in Figure 7.1 is called a *regression line* or "line of best fit" to the data points. When there is perfect correlation, all points fall exactly on the line. When data points are scattered away from the line, correlation is less than perfect, and the correlation coefficient falls between .00 and 1.00 in magnitude (ignoring signs).

When we have a perfect correlation such as that shown in Figure 7.1, we are able to predict precisely a value for one variable, given a value for the others. For example, if we know that Jason took 17 minutes for one interview, we can predict 17 minutes for a second interview. But the existence of a meaningful perfect correlation in the world around us is a relatively rare phenomenon. Most relationships investigated produce a correlation substantially less than 1.00; hence, our predictive powers are governed by the size of r.

Much can be known about correlations simply on the basis of their scattergram. The *direction* of a correlation (positive or negative) can be seen instantly by whether the scattergram slopes up or down from left to right. Figure 7.2 shows several scattergrams "idealized" by surrounding the points with a smooth envelope. You can see in Figure 7.2 that the shape of the collection of points is tied to the value of r: The fatter the scatter, the lesser the r. The extremes are when $r = \pm 1.0$ (when the scattered points fall on a straight line), and when $r = 0$ (when the scattered points fall within a circle). Correlation coefficients between 0 and 1 are associated with scattergrams that are more or less cigar shaped or oval.

When any degree of correlation exists, it is possible to run a regression line, or line of best fit, through the scattergram to represent the general relationship shown on the scattergram. Clearly the goodness of fit depends on the value of r. We use the equation for this regression line to make predictions of one variable from our knowledge of the other variable. Since one component of this equation is r, we must first consider how r is calculated.

CALCULATING THE PEARSON r

There are two basic formulas for r, a standard-score formula and a computational formula. We will examine the standard-score equation first. If we have our data for our two variables expressed in terms of Z scores (standard scores, Chapter 5), the correlation coefficient r can be determined by:

$$r = \frac{\Sigma Zx \times Zy}{N}$$

Where $Zx =$ the Z score for the X score of a pair of scores
$\quad\quad Zy =$ the Z score for the Y score of a pair of scores
$\quad\quad N =$ the number of pairs of scores

Briefly reviewing, a Z score, or standard score, is the number of standard-deviation units that a score falls above or below the mean.

To use the Z-score formula then requires that a Z score be computed for each X score, by using the mean and standard deviation for the X scores. It also requires that a Z score be computed for each Y score by using the mean and standard deviation of the Y scores. Next we compute the cross products of the Z scores and then sum them. If we divide this sum by N (and we do), we obtain the mean of the Z-score cross products. The limit of 1.00 for r is reached when the Z scores are identical within each cross-multiplied pair. When positive Z values are associated with negative Z values, the result is a negative correlation.

A more direct procedure for computing r, which sidesteps the calculation of Z scores, is called a computational, working, or raw-score formula. For *ungrouped* data this equation is:

$$r = \frac{N\Sigma XY - \Sigma X \Sigma Y}{\sqrt{[N\Sigma X^2 - (\Sigma X)^2][N\Sigma Y^2 - (\Sigma Y)^2}}$$

TABLE 7.2. Body image and eating-control scores for 29 Bulimic clients

Body image (X)	Eating control (Y)	Body image (X)	Eating control (Y)
12	16	13	15
11	13	14	13
18	17	14	17
19	19	12	14
12	12	11	14
16	15	16	14
13	14	11	13
16	17	15	21
11	14	17	17
14	19	20	18
17	20	21	19
13	17	17	14
17	19	16	17
16	14	15	17
15	14		

Where $\Sigma X=$ the sum of the X scores
$\quad\quad \Sigma Y=$ the sum of the Y scores
$\quad\quad \Sigma XY=$ the sum of the products of the X and Y scores
$\quad\quad \Sigma X^2=$ the sum of the squared X scores
$\quad\quad \Sigma Y^2=$ the sum of the squared Y scores

To illustrate the use of the computational formula, we will first demonstrate that the data in Table 7.1 form a perfect, positive relationship. If we apply the computational formula, we find that

$\Sigma X = 107$
$\Sigma Y = 107$
$\Sigma XY = 1963$
$\Sigma X^2 = 1963$
$\Sigma Y^2 = 1963$

By inserting these values into the equation,

$$r = \frac{6(1963)-(107)(107)}{\sqrt{[6(1963)-(107)^2][6(1963)-(107)^2]}}$$

$$= \frac{11778-11449}{\sqrt{[11778-11449][11778-11449]}}$$

$$= \frac{329}{\sqrt{(329)(329)}} = \frac{329}{\sqrt{(329)^2}} = \frac{329}{329} = 1.00$$

There, we did it! A useful exercise for you will be to add a number, say 1, to each of the Y scores, and leave the X scores be as they are. Then compute r again. Since correlation is concerned with *differences* among values, and not absolute values per se, you will find that r is still +1.00.

Now we will apply the raw-score formula to a set of data that more accurately reflects the size of correlations we find in actual studies. (By the way, if you actually measured intake interview times, you would not find a perfect correlation. What kind of correlation would you probably find?) This time our example data come from a study of clients involved in group therapy at a community mental-health center. The group consists of 29 persons seeking help for a weight-control condition called bulimia. As part of the therapy-evaluation program, each client was measured for several characteristics, such as locus of control, self-esteem, body image, eating control, as well as weight gain (or loss). The two scales we are concerned with are the body image and eating-control scales. Table 7.2 contains the body image and eating-control scores for each of the 29 clients.

Note in Table 7.2 that body-image scores range from 11 to 21, with the higher scores indicating a more positive body image. Eating-control scores vary from 12 to 21, with higher scores indicating better eating control. For these data in Table 7.2, the calculation of the components of the formula for r produces $\Sigma XY=7010$, $\Sigma X^2=6648$, $\Sigma Y^2=7557$, $\Sigma X=432$, and $\Sigma Y=463$. If we insert these quantities into our computational formula, we have,

$$r = \frac{29(7010) - (432)(463)}{\sqrt{[29(6648) - (432)^2][29(7557) - (463)^2]}}$$

$$= \frac{203290 - 200016}{\sqrt{[192792 - 186624][219153 - 214369]}}$$

$$= \frac{3274}{\sqrt{(6168)(4784)}} = \frac{3274}{\sqrt{29507712}}$$

$$= \frac{3274}{5432} = +.603$$

The $r = +.603$ indicates that these two variables are positively related, in that those clients with a more positive body image *tend* to be those who have better eating control. But how strong is this tendency? Given that r varies from 0 to ± 1.00 in magnitude, how do we interpret a value such as $r = .6$?

Interpretations of the magnitudes of r are sometimes as varied as the persons providing the interpretations. For now, we will say that the r of $+.60$ represents at least a moderate level of correlation. Later in this chapter and the next one we will return to a discussion of the interpretation of r.

Figure 7.3 shows a scattergram of the relationship between body image and eating control. In this example we will consider body image to be our independent variable and eating control to be our dependent variable. The question we are asking then is, "Does eating control depend on body image?" Or, "Is eating control correlated with body image?"

Note first in Figure 7.3 that the envelope surrounding the scattergram is not perfectly oval. This is how it usually is shaped when we have nonidealized data; but as we say, "It is close enough for government work." The oval-shaped envelope does clearly slope up from left to right, indicating a positive correlation.

Since body image is our independent variable, it is laid out along the abscissa. Our dependent variable, eating control, is then the ordinate variable. The lowest value for either variable is 11, so a piece of each axis was "cut out" to indicate that values less than 11 do not appear, and therefore to allow us to move our scattergram closer to the vertex (0.0 point).

THE REGRESSION EQUATION

The regression line, or line of best fit, also slopes up from left to right in Figure 7.3, as it should. The regression line can be plotted on the scattergram by applying the equation for the line. Since we are concerned with *linear* correlation, the equation for the regression line is

$$Y' = a + bX$$

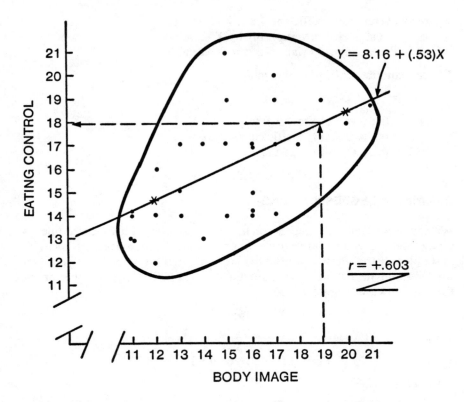

FIGURE 7.3. Scattergram of eating control and body image scores for 29 bulimic clients

where Y' = the Y value predicted from a particular X value

X = the X value used to predict Y'

b = the slope of the line, or the amount Y is increasing for each one unit increase in X

a = the point where the line intersects the Y axis

To obtain the values of the *regression coefficients, a* and *b*, we need to use the value of r and the values of the standard deviations for Y and X. We then apply the formula

$$b = r\left(\frac{Sy}{Sx}\right)$$

where r = correlation coefficient for X and Y
    Sy = the standard deviation of the Y variable
    Sx = the standard deviation of the X variable

We can compute a from the formula

$$a = \bar{Y} - b\bar{X}$$

where $\bar{Y}$ = the mean of the Y values
    b = the regression coefficient (slope)
    $\bar{X}$ = the mean of the X values

DRAWING A REGRESSION LINE

We now want to plot this regression line on our scattergram. Since the line is a straight line, all we need are two points on the line. ("The shortest distance..") A simple way to find two points is to pick two values for X and find two values for Y by applying the regression equation for each X. The specific equation for the line shown in Figure 7.3 is

$$Y' = 8.16 + (.53)x$$

If we let $X = 20$, then

$$Y' = 8.16 + (.53)20 = 8.16 + 10.6 = 18.76$$

If we let $X = 12$,

$$Y' = 8.16 + (.53)12 = 8.16 + 6.36 = 14.52$$

We now find the two points (18.76, 20) and (14.52, 12), on the scattergram, place a dot at each point, and draw a straight line through the two points.

PREDICTING A Y-SCORE

If we are given a particular X score, what Y score should be predicted? If we have drawn a regression line accurately on a scattergram, we may use it for gross predictions. We start with the given X score on the abscissa and draw a vertical line up to the regression line. Then a horizontal line is drawn over to the vertical axis (ordinate). The point at which this horizontal line intersects the ordinate is our predicted Y score for the X we began with. This procedure is depicted in Figure 7.3, where we predict a client's eating-control score given a body-image score of 19. The projection to the Y axis shows a predicted eating-control score of approximately 18.

A more accurate way to predict a Y score is to use the regression equation. If we wish to predict an eating-control score from a body-image score of 19, the regression equation would be

$$Y' = 8.16 + (.53)19$$
$$= 8.16 + 10.07$$
$$= 18.23$$

Thus, given an X score of 19, the predicted Y score is 18.23. How accurate is this prediction? Does it hold that a body-image score of 19 is always associated with an eating-control score of 18? No, not unless the r is +1.00, which it is not. As we indicated earlier, the "goodness" of a regression-equation prediction depends primarily on r. In general, the higher the r, the better the prediction. But better that what? Predictions that are based on regression equations that are built around significant r's are "better" because the use of such estimates (Y') yields more accurate predictions of a Y variable than can be made if we

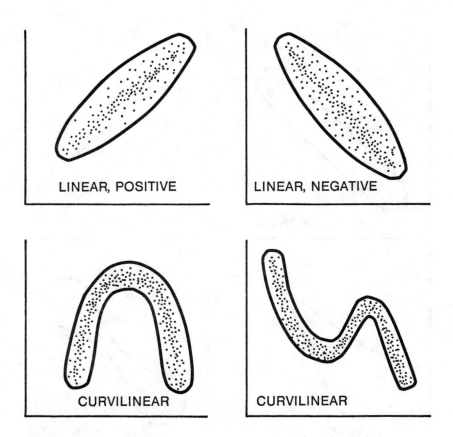

FIGURE 7.4. Illustrations of linear and curvilinear relationships

didn't have information on an X variable. Without any additional information, our best single guess for Y' is always $\bar{Y}$, the mean of the Y scores. However, if there is a significant correlation between Y and X, we can take advantage of this relationship to improve our predictive capabilities.

THE USE OF *r*

Anyone who knows how can go through the motions of determining correlation coefficients (and other statistics) and getting arithmetically correct results. However, it need not follow that such results have any meaning. Besides knowing the mathematical structure of these statistics, the user (and consumer-critic) of statistics must know when (and when not) to use statistical procedures. Mathematical ability and the use of a computer for calculations

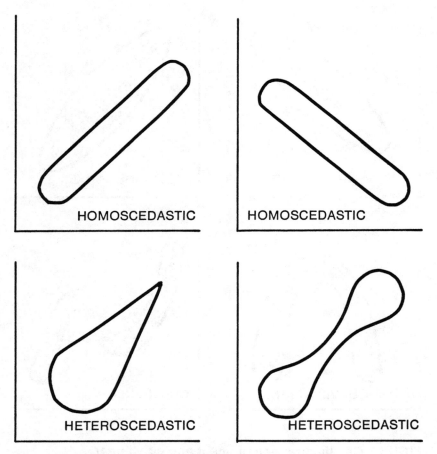

FIGURE 7.5. Illustrations of homoscedasticity and heteroscedasticity

are not substitutes for wisdom. The correlation coefficient, like other statistics we have discussed, has certain assumptions and conditions that must be met before it is used appropriately.

A first assumption for using r is that the data must be at the *interval level* of measurement. Second, the pattern of the relationship must be linear, that is, it must fall along a straight line. Third, the data must be what is called *homoscedastic*. If we measure the variances in Y for each value of X, the variances in Y at each X should be similar. This property of equal variance in Y across X bears the technical label of *homoscedasticity*.

A scattergram is very useful to give us a rough visual estimate of whether or not our data are linear and homoscedastic. If data markedly depart from linearity, as shown in Figure 7.4, the Pearson r is *not* an appropriate measure of association. If data are homoscedastic, the points will fall within a cigar shape as in Figure 7.5; marked deviations from such a shape indicate heteroscedasticity. These three assumptions, then should be met before r can be properly and fully utilized.

THE INTERPRETATION OF r

The interpretation of r can be a tricky business. Keep in mind that r is a summary index number, just as the mean and standard deviation are. As such, it is used to help describe a set of data.

The correlation coefficient r is a measure of the *linear* relationship between two interval variables. It summarizes and describes the tendency of high or low values of one variable to be regularly associated with either high or low values of the other variable. In other words, the correlation coefficient r describes the tendency of two variables to vary together (co-vary) in some consistent manner. The absolute size of the coefficient (from 0 to 1.00) indicates the strength of the tendency to co-vary. The algebraic sign tells the direction of the co-variation. Knowledge of the size and direction of r, then, permits some prediction of the value of one variable if the value of the other variable is known. For example, if $r = +.79$, our regression equation would predict a lower valued Y score given a lower valued X score.

The correlation coefficient does not tell us anything about *causality*. If two variables are related, the r does not tell us whether or not one of the variables is *causing* the variation in the other. Quite possibly some third variable is responsible for the variation in both. For example, in one midwestern state the author found a positive correlation between the number of French-speaking people in an area and the rate of child abuse in that area. But a change in one of these variables will not necessarily cause a change in the other. One is tempted, but is foolish, to conclude that it is primarily French-speaking people who are abusing children in this state. More than likely some third variable, such as population density, is causing these variables to co-vary.

Leaping to cause-and-effect statements is easy to do. It usually seems so reasonable to do so. And, in many situations, a cause-and-effect relationship may actually exist. However, a correlation coefficient *by itself* does not establish causation. Thus, r can be interpreted only in terms of association and prediction, not in terms of cause and effect.

MAGNITUDE OF r

Just how great does r have to be before we can say we have a "high" degree of relationship between two variables? Usually there are two matters that have to be considered when trying to answer this question. The first matter is concerned with probabilities, and the second matter with practical applications.

For a correlation coefficient to be useful for prediction purposes, we want that coefficient to be great enough to conclude that the coefficient is not merely a chance variant, but actually to reflect a "real" association between the variables. If we determine for a particular sample of size N that the obtained r is not likely to be a chance phenomenon, then we say that the r is *significantly different from zero*. We will present and discuss the concept of statistical significance more extensively in Chapter 8. For now, it suffices to say that a significant relationship is one that probably does not occur by chance.

A general rule to follow is that predictive confidence cannot be placed in a nonsignificant correlation. When N is small, great correlation coefficients (coefficients approaching +1.00) have a high probability of occurring by chance alone. For example, if you take two sets of three numbers ($N = 3$) and calculate r for all possible pairs, about 5 percent of the r's will be close to +1.00. For such small samples, the observation of a great r may be due solely to chance pairings of variables. When working with low Ns (N less than 25), it is best to determine the probability or likelihood that your coefficient is statistically significant before becoming ecstatic about your "high" coefficient. If the magnitude of r is such that it cannot be deemed significantly different from zero, no confidence should be placed in the coefficient as a reliable predictive tool.

As N increases, the value of r necessary to be judged significant decreases. That is, for $N = 10$, an r of .50 is quite likely to occur due to chance factors alone. However, if $N = 100$, there is less than one chance in a thousand that an r of .50 would occur solely by chance. So, in the latter case, we judge r to be significant, and in the former case, not significant.

Given that we have accepted a coefficient as representing a statistically-significant relationship between two variables, how great does a coefficient have to be before we will say it summarizes a "strong" relationship? About the only reasonable answer is that "it depends." It depends largely on what is being correlated with what, and what use is to be made of the statistic once it has been calculated.

Guilford (1950, p. 165) has offered the following descriptive scale in a partial attempt to answer the question of how "large" a coefficient must be to be called "big":

Absolute magnitude of coefficient	Degree of relationship
Less than .20	Slight, almost negligible
.20 - .40	Low correlation, relationship definite but little
.40 - .70	Moderate correlation, substantial relationship
.70 - .90	High correlation, marked relationship
.90 - 1.00	Very high correlation, very dependable relationship

These descriptive interpretations apply only if the correlation coefficient is great enough to be considered statistically significant. A relationship that is likely to be due solely to chance variation is unworthy of being identified further. Although Guilford's framework is generally acceptable, there is a strong practical component to our judgment of how "high" is "high" enough. For some investigative situations, an obtained correlation as low as .30 - .40 will lead the investigator(s) to celebrate. In other research areas, a coefficient as great as .70 - .80 would cause depression to set in. How high should r be for what you are interested in researching? Once again, it depends on the specific case.

Another way to view the importance of the value of r is to determine the extent to which a correlation improves our prediction over guessing. Remember, if we are trying to predict some Y, our best estimate is $\overline{Y}$, assuming that we have no additional information. However, if there is *any* correlation between Y and another variable X ($r \neq 0$), then this correlation is of *some* value because it will reduce to some extent the amount of discrepancy inherent in our predictions. The *coefficient* of *determination*, r^2, tells us how much reduction is effected by the use of r. The coefficient of determination (r^2) tells us the proportion of variance in variable Y that is associated with variance in variable X. Such variance is called common variance, and this variance held in common can be considered to be determined or caused by the same factors. For example, suppose we know that the number of treatment hours for clients in therapy is related to self-esteem scores, with an $r = .50$. If we square .50, we get .25. If we now want to predict treatment hours from self-esteem scores, we much recognize we can only predict 25% of the variance in treatment hours. The other 75% is *independent* of self-esteem scores and cannot be predicted by the self-esteem instrument. Now, suppose r is only .30. Then $r^2 = .09$, and we are able to account for only 9% of the variance in treatment hours by using our self-esteem instrument.

Obviously, the lower the r, the lower the r^2, and the less our improvement in prediction over that of merely guessing. Depending on the particular situation, the level of r^2 reaches a point where the game is not worth the candle. That is, r and r^2 are of such a low value that poor predictions are not worth the costs involved in practical situations. For example, administering and scoring instruments (such as measures of self-esteem) during intake procedures require time and money. If the use of an instrument does not improve predictability of outcome measures over that of guessing or flipping a coin, the value to be gained by using the instrument is probably less than the costs involved.

Some concluding comments concerning the interpretation of r. When one compares an r of .60 to an r of .30, the tendency is to think of the r of .60 as being twice as strong a correlation as the r of .30; but that is not the case. The correlation coefficient is not on a ratio scale, but the coefficient of determination (r^2) is. Thus, two variables that are correlated with $r = .60$ have four times ($.6^2 = .36$) as much common variance as two variables correlated with $r = .30$ ($.30^2 = .09$) have. Finally, it is important to remember that it is the magnitude of r and not the direction that determines the strength of a relationship. A correlation of $-.60$ is stronger than one of $+.50$, and an r of $-.40$ and an r of $+.40$ are equivalent in associative strength.

THE SPEARMAN RANK-ORDER COEFFICIENT OF CORRELATION

Quite often data collected by social work investigators conform only to the properties of an ordinal scale. Ordinal data should not be used to calculate a Pearson r, since one of the basic assumptions for using this statistic is interval scaling. The technique commonly used to correlate ordinal data is called the Spearman rank-order correlation coefficient. We will symbolize this statistic by r_s. The Spearman coefficient is much easier to calculate than the Pearson coefficient. The equation for r_s can be derived from the equation for r; hence the Spearman coefficient is a special case of the Pearson coefficient. Whereas we typically prefer to have 30 or more cases for computing r, r_s is most often used when the number of pairs of scores is less than 30. The Spearman r_s can be used for both ordinal and interval data, and when both coefficients are calculated for the same data (interval), the two values will be very similar.

Data of an ordinal nature come from many different places in social work practice. Client evaluation forms, worker performance evaluations, and the like, often provide ordinal data. As indicated earlier, many social work research endeavors utilize ordinal as well as nominal and interval data. Our purpose here is to show how the Spearman r_s is calculated and then interpreted.

Our example problem comes from the study of police officers mentioned in Chapter 6. The first variable is a *rating* from 1 to 10 on how supportive officers believe the public to be with respect to their departments' policy on handling domestic-disturbance calls. A rating of 1 indicates no support, and a rating of 10 indicates full support. The second variable is the length of time in minutes, on the average, the officer spends on each domestic-disturbance call. The question of interest here is whether or not the amount of time spent on a call depends on or is related to the degree of perceived support by the public.

Table 7.3 presents the rating and time scores for 15 officers randomly selected from the larger sample of 194 presented in Chapter 6. Table 7.3 also contains an illustration of the steps necessary to calculate r_s. The first data column represents the public support ratings by officers A through O. The next column shows the time in minutes per call for each of the same officers.

To compute r_s, both of these scores must be converted to ordinal scales by *ranking* the scores. For the public-support scores the highest rating is assigned a rank of "1," the next highest support score a rank of "2," and so on. If we have tied scores, as we do here, we assign to the tied score the *average* of the ranks they would have received had they not been tied. Thus, both of the public-support scores of 6 receive a ranking of 5.5, the average of the rankings of 5 and 6. The three support scores of 1 each receive a ranking of 14, the average of ranks 13, 14, and 15. The next data column in Table 7.3 shows the rankings for the time scores, with the highest time of 60 minutes assigned a rank of 1 and the lowest time of 5 minutes assigned a rank of 15. Note that the last assigned rank is equal to N, the number of pairs of scores, unless the last ranked score is tied with one or more other scores (as it was for the support scores).

You are reminded here that, just as for computation of r, the data *must* appear as matched pairs of scores. Also, you should exercise caution in assigning ranks, especially if there are tied scores. Generally, if the last assigned rank is equal to the number of scores being ranked (N), it is a reasonably good indication that the ranking was done properly.

The next computational step is to *subtract* each pair of ranks. In our example, we subtract the rank for time scores from the rank for support scores. The results of these subtractions are in the column headed D in Table 7.3. We then take the process one step further and *square* the differences in ranks, or we square D to obtain a value of D^2. These squared differences are shown in Table 7.3 in the D^2 column.

The formula for the calculation of r_s is

$$r_s = 1 - \left[\frac{6(\Sigma D^2)}{N(N^2 - 1)} \right]$$

where ΣD^2 = the sum of the squared differences in ranks
N = the number of pairs of ranks

It is fairly easy to see how a correlation of +1.0 would be obtained. If both members of each pair of ranks were identical, each number in the D column would be zero, and the fraction in the equation for r_s would equal zero. Thus, in this case, $r_s = 1 - 0 = 1.0$. We have learned to associate this value with a *perfect-positive correlation*. If the ranks in both columns were the opposite of each other, that is, in inverse order, the expression $6(\Sigma D^2)$ would be just twice

TABLE 7.3 Calculation of the Spearman r_s for ratings of public support and length of time on spouse-abuse calls for 15 officers

Officer	Public support rating	Time on call in minutes	Public support rank	Time spent rank	D	D^2
A	6	30	5.5	4.5	1	1.0
B	7	5	4	15	−11	121.0
C	5	10	7.5	14	− 6.5	42.25
D	2	20	11.5	9.5	2.0	4.0
E	5	30	7.5	4.5	3.0	9.0
F	10	15	1	12.5	−11.5	132.25
G	6	15	5.5	12.5	− 7.0	49.0
H	2	20	11.5	9.5	2.0	4.0
I	1	20	14	9.5	4.5	20.25
J	1	45	14	2	12.0	144.0
K	1	60	14	1	13.0	169.0
L	9	30	2	4.5	− 2.5	6.25
M	8	20	3	9.5	− 6.5	−42.25
N	3	25	10	7	3	9
O	4	30	9	4.5	4.5	20.25

$$\Sigma D^2 = 773.50$$

$$r_s = 1 - \left[\frac{6(\Sigma D^2)}{N(N^2-1)}\right] = 1 - \left[\frac{6(773.5)}{15(225-1)}\right]$$

$$= 1 - \left[\frac{4641}{3360}\right]$$

$$= 1 - 1.38$$

$$= -.38$$

as great as the expression $N(N^2-1)$, and the fraction would have the value of 2. The subtraction, then, would produce $r_s = 1-2 = -1$, or the value we have come to associate with perfect *inverse,* or *negative,* correlation.

The details of the computation of r_s for our example are shown in Table 7.3. The resulting r_s coefficient is −.38. The fact that the correlation between public support and time scores is negative can be seen simply by inspecting the pairs of ranks. The higher ranks on one variable tend to be associated with the lower ranks on the other. The "strength" of the association between the two variables is estimated, as with the Pearson r, by the proximity of the calculated coefficient to the "perfect" coefficient (+1). Here, a coefficient of −.38

represents a "moderate" relationship between the two variables, at best. Thus, we can conclude that the time spent by police officers on spouse-abuse calls is moderately related to their perceived degree of support by the public they serve. The *direction* of the relationship (−) indicates that those who perceive the greater amount of public support *tend* to be those who spend the lesser amounts of time in dealing with disturbance calls.

The existence of a large number of tied scores can have the effect of spuriously exaggerating the magnitude of r_s. However, it has been shown that it takes many scores of the same value (six or seven) before "correction factors" need be applied. Since we usually use r_s when N is low ($N < 30$ or so), in actual practice it is relatively rare for so many scores to be tied for a single rank. If there should be a need to apply such an adjustment to r_s, the procedure can be found in Siegel (1956, pp. 206-210).

Chapter 8

Tests of Statistical Significance

Earlier in this book (Chapter 5) we talked about statistics and parameters. A *statistic* is a numerical description of a set of data that is defined by an investigator to be a *sample* from some population, and a *parameter* is a numerical description of scores that an investigator determines to be all of the relevant scores for analysis, that is, a total *population* of scores. We defined the *mean* for a set of scores as the arithmetic average of the scores. If the set of scores is considered a sample, then the mean is called a statistic for that sample. If the set of scores comprises a population, then the mean is termed a parameter. As we indicated earlier, many times all we are interested in is describing a set of data in hand, whether it be called a sample or a population. But if we wish to extend our statistical descriptions beyond our in-hand data, then we are generalizing from a sample to a larger population of scores. We are then entering into the province of inferential statistics.

A basic question involved when we use inferential statistics is, "knowing what I do about the numerical characteristics of a smaller set of data (sample), what can I say or conclude about the numerical characteristics of a larger set of data (the population the sample came from)?" To answer this question, we apply to our data what are called *tests of statistical significance,* or merely *tests of significance*. In this chapter we will describe four such tests of significance: the Chi-square (χ^2) test, the Pearson r test, the Spearman r_s test, and the Student t test. These particular tests of significance are frequently used by social work investigators in practice.

When we use these tests of significance, we assume that the data in hand constitute a *sample* from a larger population of data of interest. Keep in mind that we are referring to a population of score values, not necessarily a population of people. We further assume that the sample is *representative* of the larger population, in such manner that the sample characteristics accurately reflect relevant population characteristics. If we use appropriate procedures in selecting our samples, we can determine the degree of representativeness of our samples.

CHI-SQUARE (χ^2) TEST OF INDEPENDENCE

In Chapter 6 we saw how two (or more) variables can be cross tabulated in a manner that produces the joint-frequency distribution for the two variables. We then discussed several ways in which we can determine and describe the existence and extent of any observed relationship between the two variables. For example, we used epsilon and several Chi-square derivatives to determine whether or not variables are associated with or dependent on each other.

Several key points were made in Chapter 6 that will be re-emphasized here. We will usually find in our research data that two variables are related or associated *to some degree*; we rarely observe complete independence between two variables in a sample. This means that whenever we do a crosstab and compute row percentages (or column percentages), we usually find that sets of row percentages (or column percentages), are *not* equivalent. Hence, we typically can conclude from sample data that how one variable is distributed depends on how a second variable is distributed.

We need some measure of the stability of our observed associations. Are the associations chance findings, that is, can we attribute row percentage differences to chance fluctuations? If we consider our data in hand to be a sample and if we observe an association on the sample data, can we *infer* that an association also exists in the population from which the sample was drawn? Or, is it possible or likely that *no* association exists in the population, and that any association we find in our sample data is due to sampling error.

Chi-square is a useful measure for determining the probability or likelihood that a particular sample joint-frequency distribution was derived from a population where an association does not exist. That is, the two variables are *independent* of each other in the population, and any association observed in the sample is due to sampling error. If we determine that our sample association did not come from a population where the variables are independent, then the sample must have come from a population where the two variables are in fact related.

Consider once again the crosstab presented in Table 6.7. The question we asked of these data is whether or not the use of a weapon in a domestic-violence situation *depends* on whether or not a client is a welfare recipient. We determined that Cramer's V = .207 and concluded that a weak to moderate association exists for this sample of 57 clients. But does this observed association also exist for the larger population of domestic-violence shelter clients?

Our method for answering this question requires that we first establish what is called a "null hypothesis." Our null hypothesis for this situation is that two variables are *independent* of each other in the population. If the null hypothesis is actually true, then any association observed in the sample is the result of sampling error. If the null hypothesis is in fact not true, then our sample association reflects some actual degree of association in the population.

The value of Chi-square is used to determine the probability that the null hypothesis is true. Generally speaking, the larger the computed Chi-square, the less the probability that the null hypothesis is true. How do we interpret the value of χ^2? If the null hypothesis is true, how often can we have sample data that will produce a Chi-square of a given magnitude, or larger, just by chance alone? In other words, we want to know if our observed χ^2 is statistically significant. If χ^2 is found to be statistically significant, then we can conclude that our observed association is not likely to be due to sampling error, and we will reject our null hypothesis. If χ^2 is judged *not to be* statistically significant, then we will attribute our observed sample association to chance factors and retain our null hypothesis.

The computed χ^2 for Table 6.7 is 2.45 (see Chapter 6 for the computation of χ^2). How do we interpret the value of 2.45? First, we must determine what is known as the *degrees of freedom* (*df*) for these data. To determine the *df* for an R x C (rows by columns) table like Table 6.7, we use the formula $(r-1)(C-1)$. In this case, $(2-1)(2-1)=1$. A 3 x 3 table would have $(3-1)(3-1)=4$ *df*. How many *df* for a 3 x 2 table? Once again, $df=(R-1)(C-1)$, where R and C refer to the number of rows and columns.

We then take our observed $\chi^2=2.45$ with 1 *df* and look at Table 8.1. The first column of Table 8.1 lists *df*s from 1 to 30. The next five columns are headed by five different *significance levels* (often denoted α). The significance levels vary from $\alpha=.10$ to $\alpha=.001$. Let's concentrate first on the .05 and .01 significance levels for a χ^2 with 1 *df*. The value 3.84 can be interpreted in the following manner: If the null hypothesis is true (independence), then the probability of observing a sample χ^2 *as great as 3.84 or greater* is 5% (.05) or less. Similarly, if the null hypothesis is true, the likelihood of getting a sample χ^2 of *6.64 or greater* is 1% (.01) or less. If we observe a sample χ^2 greater than these values, then it is not very likely that the null hypothesis is true, and we would opt for the alternative, that an association exists in the population.

It is a generally accepted convention that we will not reject a null hypothesis unless there is less than a 5% chance that it is, in fact, true. (Some researchers require that this probability be less than 1%.) Another way of saying this is that we will not reject a null hypothesis unless there is at least a 95% chance that it is false.

In our example from Table 6.7, the observed χ^2 of 2.45 is less than the tabled value of 3.84. We can conclude that there is greater than a 5% chance that the null hypothesis is correct, so we will accept or retain it. Retaining the null hypothesis in this case means that there is a reasonable chance that our two variables are *independent* of each other in the population, even though we observe dependency in the sample data. Thus, we can say that our sample χ^2 is not significant at the 5% level of significance, and our observed weak to moderate association is probably due to chance sampling factors.

In Chapter 6 we also presented and discussed the association between Type of Report and Year of Report for the child-abuse registry data (see Table 6.9). We found a moderate to weak relationship between these two variables in our sample of 6,211 cases. Is this observed association due merely to sampling error, or does it represent a real association between these variables in the population?

TABLE 8.1. Chi-Square Distribution*

df	.10	.05	.02	.01	.001
			α levels		
1	2.71	3.84	5.41	6.64	10.83
2	4.60	5.99	7.82	9.21	13.82
3	6.25	7.82	9.84	11.34	16.27
4	7.78	9.49	11.67	13.28	18.46
5	9.24	11.07	13.39	15.09	20.52
6	10.64	12.59	15.03	16.81	22.46
7	12.02	14.07	16.62	18.48	24.32
8	13.36	15.51	18.17	20.09	26.12
9	14.68	16.92	19.68	21.67	27.88
10	15.99	18.31	21.16	23.21	29.59
11	17.28	19.68	22.62	24.72	31.26
12	18.55	21.03	24.05	26.22	32.91
13	19.81	22.36	25.47	27.69	34.53
14	21.06	23.68	26.87	29.14	36.12
15	22.31	25.00	28.26	30.58	37.70
16	23.54	26.30	29.63	32.00	39.25
17	24.77	27.59	31.00	33.41	40.79
18	25.99	28.87	32.35	34.80	42.31
19	27.20	30.14	33.69	36.19	43.82
20	28.41	31.41	35.02	37.57	45.32
21	29.62	32.67	36.34	38.93	46.80
22	30.81	33.92	37.66	40.29	48.27
23	32.01	35.17	38.97	41.64	49.73
24	33.20	36.42	40.27	42.98	51.18
25	34.38	37.65	41.57	44.31	52.62
26	35.56	38.88	42.86	45.64	54.05
27	36.74	40.11	44.14	46.96	55.48
28	37.92	41.34	45.42	48.28	56.89
29	39.09	42.56	46.69	49.59	58.30
30	40.26	43.77	47.96	50.89	59.70

*To be significant the X^2 obtained from the data must be equal to or greater than the value shown in the table.

Table 8.1 is taken from Table IV of Fisher and Yates: *Statistical Tables for Biological, Agricultural and Medical Research,* published by Longman Group Ltd., London. (Previously published by Oliver & Boyd Ltd., Edinburgh), and by permission of the authors and publishers.

The χ^2 for Table 6.9 data is equal to 296.28, with $df=8$ $(df=(5-)(3-1))$. When we refer to Table 8.1, we see that our observed χ^2 exceeds the tabled values for both the 5% and 1% significance levels (15.51 and 20.09). In fact, we also exceed by far the value for the .1% level of significance. Since we have *exceeded* the tabled values, we judge our χ^2 to be statistically significant and *reject* the null hypothesis of no association. We can conclude that there is less than a .1% chance our finding of association is due merely to sampling error. We are extremely confident, in this case, that the association observed in our sample also exists in the population of these child-abuse registry cases.

Let's summarize the process of hypothesis testing described so far. First we establish a null hypothesis of no association in a population. Then we observe our sample data and calculate χ^2 and df. After that we enter a table like Table 8.1 and determine if we exceed the critical value of χ^2 for a given significance level ($\alpha=.05$ or .01). If we exceed the tabled value for a particular significance level, we can reject the null hypothesis at that level; if we do not exceed the tabled value, we can accept or retain the null hypothesis at that level. What if we had a $\chi^2=8.17$ for $df=2$? What decision do we reach with respect to the null hypothesis? We note that χ^2 is significant at the 5% significance level but not at the 1% level. So we could reject the null hypothesis at the 5% level, but retain it at the 1% level. If we reject a null hypothesis at the 5% significance level, does that mean that the null hypothesis is definitely not true? No! We can never disprove the null hypothesis in an absolute sense from sample data. The best we can do is state the likelihood that it is not true (e.g., less than 5%). So rejecting at the 5% level means there is less than a 5% chance that the null hypothesis is correct. Accordingly, there is also a 5% chance or less that our decision to reject is wrong. If we reject at the 1% level, then there is a 1% chance (or less) that our decision is wrong. To say our decision may be wrong here means that we may have rejected a null hypothesis that is true. To make this kind of error, is to make what is called a Type-I error. The probability of making a Type-I error is determined by the significance level at which the null hypothesis was rejected. If you reject at the 5% level, the probability of a Type-I error is 5% or less. If you reject at the 1% level, the probability is 1% or less. Generally speaking, if you reject at the k level of significance, the probability of a Type-I error is k or less.

Some Important Points About Chi-Square

Whenever we have a 2 x 2 crosstab (where $df=1$), and especially when any cell expected frequency is relatively small (less than 10), the computation of X^2 requires an adjustment factor. The reason for this adjustment will not be discussed here (see Blalock, 1979).

The following is a general formula that incorporates what is called Yates' correction:

$$\chi^2 = \Sigma \frac{(|O-E|-.5)^2}{E}$$

where $|O-E|$ is the absolute value of the difference between observed and expected frequencies for each table cell.

When we have cases where expected frequencies are very small (less than 5), even Yates' correction can produce a misleading decision. We then use a technique known as Fisher's exact test. See Blalock (1979) for the details of this procedure.

One last point to consider is cell collapsing. Even if N and df are great, we may encounter a situation in which cells have a small value of E. Instead of applying Yates' correction, we can collapse or combine cells to increase the observed frequencies (Os) in these cells. This can be done as long as the collapsing procedure makes sense in terms of the research problem.

TESTING THE SIGNIFICANCE OF r

In Chapter 7 we introduced the Pearson r as a measure of the linear correlation between two interval scaled variables. We saw that the magnitude of r varies from 0.0 to 1.0, and that one of the important uses of r is for making predictions. It was pointed out that for a correlation coefficient to be useful for prediction purposes, the coefficient must be large enough to be judged *statistically significant*. Our task here is to outline the procedure for determining whether or not a particular r is significant. The process is similar to that for testing the significance of χ^2.

We start with a sample of data for which we have measured r for two variables. The question then becomes, "Given the magnitude of a sample r, what can we say, and with what degree of certainty, about the correlation coefficient for these two variables in the population?" Is there a "real" correlation in the population? Or is the correlation actually zero in the population, and our sample r is just a chance finding?

The null hypothesis is that there is a zero correlation between the two variables, or population $r = O$. We then determine the degrees of freedom associated with r. For r, $df = N - 2$, where N equals the number of *pairs* of scores. We next take our obtained sample r and df and refer to a table like Table 8.2. The first column indicates dfs varying from 1 to 100. The next five columns are headed by five significance levels (.1 to .001). The body of the table contains critical values of r that must be exceeded to reject the null hypothesis at a given significance level.

In Chapter 7 we calculated an $r = .603$ for the body-image and eating-control scores of 29 bulimic persons. A correlation of this magnitude can be described as "moderate," indicating a substantial relationship. For 29 cases, the $df = N - 2 = 29 - 2 = 27$. Note in Table 8.2 that a $df = 27$ does not appear. This will require us to "interpolate" between the critical rs associated with dfs of 25 and 30. Our obtained r of .603 exceeds all of the tabled critical values for this df, so we can reject the null hypothesis of $r = 0$ in the population at the .1% level of significance. We can conclude that it is not very likely that our observed correlation is merely a chance finding. Rather, we are on firm

TABLE 8.2. Critical values for Pearson product-moment correlation coefficients, _r_

df	.1	.05	.02	.01	.001
	α Levels (Two-Tailed Test)				
1	.98769	.99692	.999507	.999877	.9999988
2	.90000	.95000	.98000	.990000	.99900
3	.8054	.8783	.93433	.95873	.99116
4	.7293	.8114	.8822	.91720	.97406
5	.6694	.7545	.8329	.8745	.95074
6	.6215	.7067	.7887	.8343	.92493
7	.5822	.6664	.7498	.7977	.8982
8	.5494	.6319	.7155	.7646	.8721
9	.5214	.6021	.6851	.7348	.8371
10	.4973	.5760	.6581	.7079	.8233
11	.4762	.5529	.6339	.6835	.8010
12	.4575	.5324	.6120	.6614	.7800
13	.4409	.5139	.5923	.6411	.7603
14	.4259	.4973	.5742	.6226	.7420
15	.4124	.4821	.5577	.6055	.7246
16	.4000	.4683	.5425	.5897	.7084
17	.3887	.4555	.5285	.5751	.6932
18	.3783	.4438	.5155	.5614	.6787
19	.3687	.4329	.5034	.5487	.6652
20	.3598	.4227	.4921	.5368	.6524
25	.3233	.3809	.4451	.4869	.5974
30	.2960	.3494	.4093	.4487	.5541
35	.2746	.3246	.3810	.4182	.5189
40	.2573	.3044	.3578	.3932	.4896
45	.2428	.2875	.3384	.3721	.4648
50	.2306	.2732	.3218	.3541	.4433
60	.2108	.2500	.2948	.3248	.4078
70	.1954	.2319	.2737	.3017	.3799
80	.1829	.2172	.2565	.2830	.3568
90	.1726	.2050	.2422	.2673	.3375
100	.1638	.1946	.2301	.2540	.3211
	.05	.025	.01	.005	.0005
	α Levels (One-Tailed Test)				

Table 8.2 is taken from Table VII of Fisher & Yates: _Statistical Tables for Biological, Agricultural and Medical Research,_ published by Longman Group Ltd., London. (Previously published by Oliver and Boyd Ltd., Edinburgh), and by permission of the authors and publishers.

ground that a non-zero correlation between these two variables does in fact exist in the population from which the 29 cases were drawn.

As another example, assume an astute social worker measured the correlation between length of time a family remained on Aid to Families with Dependent Children (AFDC) and the amount of the monthly check. For 42 families, the obtained r was found to be equal to .271. Is this value of r, for this sample size, significantly different from zero? Once again we use Table 8.2. The $df = 42 - 2 = 40$. We find our obtained value of .271 does not exceed .304, the critical value of r that must be exceeded to reject the null hypothesis at the 5% level of significance. There is better than a 5% chance our null hypothesis is true, so we will accept it and conclude that our sample r is *not significantly different from zero,* and could very well be a chance finding. We can further state that there is *not* a statistically significant relationship between length of time on AFDC and the amount of the monthly check.

The next example illustrates the fact that it is the magnitude of r that determines significance, and not the sign of r. For the bulimic study presented earlier, a correlation of $-.49$ was obtained for self-esteem and body-image scores for 32 clients. In this study the lower the self-esteem score, the greater the self-esteem. The r of $-.49$ indicates that those with better self-esteem *tend* to have the better body image. Inspection of Table 8.2 shows that this correlation is significantly different from zero at the 1% level of significance (critical $r = .4487$, $df = 30$). We conclude that body image and self-esteem are correlated in the population. The probability of being wrong in stating this conclusion is our significance level (1% or less), or the probability of making a Type-I error. Later in this chapter we will address Type-II errors, or the probability of retaining a false null hypothesis.

It is important to note in Table 8.2 that as df increases, the critival value of r necessary for rejecting the null hypothesis decreases. This means that for small samples we need large rs to have correlations significantly different from zero. For large samples, small rs may turn out to be statistically significant. Once again, to say that a finding (χ^2, r) is statistically significant is only to say that the particular finding is not likely to be a chance finding. Statistical significance does not mean the same as theoretical or practical significance. A "significant" correlation may be low enough in magnitude to be judged relatively useless in terms of predictive power.

TESTING THE SIGNIFICANCE OF rs

Determining the statistical significance of the rank-order correlation coefficient rs involves much the same process as that for the Pearson r. One establishes a null hypothesis that $rs = 0$ in the population, obtains a sample rs, and refers the obtained rs to a table of critical rs. As an illustration, we found in Chapter 7 that the amount of time spend on spouse-abuse calls by police officers is moderately related $(rs = -.38)$ to the perceived degree of support by the public they serve. For rs, $df = N - 1$, were $N =$ the number of pairs of scores.

Table 8.3 contains critical values for *rs* for the 5% and 1% levels of significance. For our sample of 15 police officers, $df = N - 1$ or $15 - 1 = 14$. Since $df = 14$ is not listed in Table 8.3, we must interpolate between values listed for $df = 13$ and $df = 15$. Our approximate critical *rs* for the 5% and 1% levels are .521 and .657. Our obtained value of $-.38$ clearly does not exceed .521, so we do not reject the null hypothesis. We conclude that, while we observe a moderate correlation between these variables in the sample, this correlation is not significantly different from zero. It is quite possible that the variables are not related at all in the population of police officers.

TESTING THE SIGNIFICANCE OF THE DIFFERENCE IN MEANS

The statistical significance tests outlined so far have been concerned with assessing the likelihood that *sample relationships* have occurred by chance. Our next procedure concerns a situation where we have *two* samples of scores from which we have obtained means for the same variable. For example, we might have two groups of clients for which we have measured self-esteem. We can ask whether the mean self-esteem score for one group ($\bar{X}_1$) differs significantly from the mean for the other group ($\bar{X}_2$). Or, can the difference we observe in the two sample means be attributed to sampling error or chance factors?

As another example, suppose we have constructed a 30-item scale to measure "administrative style." The higher the score on the scale, the more humanocratic the administrator. We obtain responses to our instrument from 22 administrators of private agencies and from 20 administrators in public agencies. We speculate *a priori* that administrators in these two types of agencies differ in administrator style *as measured by our instrument*. After coding and analyzing our data, we find that the mean-scale score for private agencies is $\bar{X}_1 = 23.1$, and the mean scale for public is $\bar{X}_2 = 20.7$. Is there a difference in "style" scores for these two groups? Yes, 23.1 is greater than 20.7. If all that we were interested in were these two *samples,* then our job is done. But we typically use sample data (in this case, means) to infer something about populations that samples are drawn from. So we want to compare sample means and, on the basis of an observed difference, infer something about the difference in population means. In this situation we want to know whether or not the population of private-agency administrators and the population of public-agency administrators *differ* in their administrative style.

To determine whether or not a difference exists in population means, we follow a process similar to that for χ^2 and *r*. The null hypothesis is that the mean "style" scores for the two populations are equal. If the null hypothesis is true, then any difference we observe in sample means is due to sampling error or other chance factors.

We then calculate what is called the *t*-statistic. The generic equation for *t* is

$$t = \frac{\bar{X}_1 - \bar{X}_2}{S_{\bar{X}_1 - \bar{X}_2}}$$

where $\bar{X}_1$ = the mean of the first sample
$\bar{X}_2$ = the mean of the second sample
and $S_{\bar{x}_1 - \bar{x}_2}$ = the standard error of the difference between means

It is important to note that "$S_{\bar{x}_1 - \bar{x}_2}$" is a symbol and not an operation. The formula for $S_{\bar{x}_1 - \bar{x}_2}$ is

$$S_{\bar{x}_1 - \bar{x}_2} = \sqrt{\left(\frac{\Sigma X_1^2 - \dfrac{(\Sigma X_1)^2}{N_1} + \Sigma X_2^2 - \dfrac{(\Sigma X_2)^2}{N_2}}{N_1 + N_2 - 2}\right)\left(\frac{1}{N_1} + \frac{1}{N_2}\right)}$$

where X_1 = any score in sample one N_1 = number of scores in sample one
X_2 = any score in sample two N_2 = number of scores in sample two

TABLE 8.3. Critical values of the rank-order correlation coefficient for testing $H_o: p = 0$

		Level of significance for 1-tailed test			
		.05	.025	.005	.0005
	df	Level of significance for 2-tailed test			
N	N − 1	.10	.05	.01	.001
5	4	.900	1.000	—	—
6	5	.829	.886	1.000	—
7	6	.714	.786	.929	1.000
8	7	.643	.738	.881	.976
9	8	.600	.700	.833	.933
10	9	.564	.648	.794	.903
12	11	.503	.587	.727	.846
14	13	.464	.538	.679	.802
16	15	.429	.503	.635	.762
18	17	.401	.472	.600	.728
20	19	.380	.447	.570	.696
22	21	.361	.425	.544	.667
24	23	.344	.406	.521	.642
26	25	.331	.390	.501	.619
28	27	.317	.375	.483	.598
30	29	.306	.362	.467	.580
40	39	.264	.313	.405	.507
60	59	.214	.255	.331	.418
100	99	.165	.197	.257	.326

Adapted from Zar, J. 1972. Significance testing of the Spearman rank-correlation coefficient. J. Am. Stat. Assoc. **67:**578-580. Reprinted by permission of the author and publisher.

TABLE 8.4. The t Distribution*

df	.2	.1	.05	.02	.01	.001
				α Levels for Two-Tailed Test		
1	3.078	6.314	12.706	31.821	63.657	636.619
2	1.886	2.920	4.303	6.965	9.925	31.598
3	1.638	2.353	3.182	4.541	5.841	12.924
4	1.533	2.132	2.776	3.747	4.604	8.610
5	1.476	2.015	2.571	3.365	4.032	6.869
6	1.440	1.943	2.447	3.143	3.707	5.959
7	1.415	1.895	2.365	2.998	3.499	5.408
8	1.397	1.860	2.306	2.896	3.355	5.041
9	1.383	1.833	2.262	2.821	3.250	4.781
10	1.372	1.812	2.228	2.764	3.169	4.587
11	1.363	1.796	2.201	2.718	3.106	4.437
12	1.356	1.782	2.179	2.681	3.055	4.318
13	1.350	1.771	2.160	2.650	3.012	4.221
14	1.345	1.761	2.145	2.624	2.977	4.140
15	1.341	1.753	2.131	2.602	2.947	4.073
16	1.337	1.746	2.120	2.583	2.921	4.015
17	1.333	1.740	2.110	2.567	2.898	3.965
18	1.330	1.734	2.101	2.552	2.878	3.922
19	1.328	1.729	2.093	2.539	2.861	3.883
20	1.325	1.725	2.086	2.528	2.845	3.850
21	1.323	1.721	2.080	2.518	2.831	3.819
22	1.321	1.717	2.074	2.508	2.819	3.792
23	1.319	1.714	2.069	2.500	2.807	3.767
24	1.318	1.711	2.064	2.492	2.797	3.745
25	1.316	1.708	2.060	2.485	2.787	3.725
26	1.315	1.706	2.056	2.479	2.779	3.707
27	1.314	1.703	2.052	2.473	2.771	3.690
28	1.313	1.701	2.048	2.467	2.763	3.674
29	1.311	1.699	2.045	2.462	2.756	3.659
30	1.310	1.697	2.042	2.457	2.750	3.646
40	1.303	1.684	2.021	2.423	2.704	3.551
60	1.296	1.671	2.000	2.390	2.660	3.460
120	1.289	1.658	1.980	2.358	2.617	3.373
∞	1.282	1.645	1.960	2.326	2.576	3.291
	.10	.05	.025	.01	.005	.0005
			Levels for a One-Tailed Test			

*To be significant, the t obtained from the data must be equal to or greater than the value shown in the table.

Table 8.4 is taken from Table III of Fisher & Yates: *Statistical Tables for Biological, Agricultural and Medical Research,* published by Longman Group Ltd., London. (Previously published by Oliver and Boyd Ltd., Edinburgh), and by permission of the authors and publishers.

While this formula appears ominous at first glance, it still remains so after a second and third glance. It is not as important that you memorize this formula as it is that you understand what it signifies. The standard error of the difference in means is, for the most part, a measure of sampling error. So in the t-test formula, we are dividing a difference in sample means by a measure of sampling error.

Let's assume that $S_{\bar{x}_1 - \bar{x}_2} = 1.1$ for our example problem. Then

$$t = \frac{\bar{X}_1 - \bar{X}_2}{S_{\bar{x}_1 - \bar{x}_2}} = \frac{2.4}{1.1} = 2.18$$

The df associated with t is computed by

$$df = N_1 + N_2 - 2 = 22 + 20 - 2 = 42 - 2 = 40$$

We take our obtained t and df and enter a table like Table 8.4. Table 8.4 contains critical values of t necessary to reject the null hypothesis at various significance levels and dfs.

For $df = 40$, the critical values of t at the 5% and 1% significance levels are $t = 2.021$ and $t = 2.704$. Our obtained t falls between these two critical values, so we can reject the null hypothesis at the 5% level, but retain it at the 1% level. If we do decide to reject at the 5% level, we can conclude that administrative-style scores are significantly different for the two types of administrators. The probability of this conclusion being wrong is 5% or less (Type-I error).

In the study of police officers we have used for examples (see Appendix A), respondents indicated whether or not they saw themselves as mediators in spouse-abuse cases. Are "mediators" older or younger than "nonmediators"? Do "mediators" spend more or less time on spouse-abuse call than do "nonmediators"? We can use t-tests to answer these two questions.

For the first question, the mean age of mediators is $\bar{X}_1 = 31.7$ years and for nonmediators $\bar{X}_2 = 34.7$ years. The difference in means is -3.0 years, $S_{\bar{x}_1 - \bar{x}_2}$ was found to equal 1.13 and $df = 183$. So

$$t = \frac{31.7 - 34.7}{1.13} = -2.65$$

When we refer to Table 8.4, we use the $df = \alpha$ value, since $df > 120$. We ignore the sign of the t and find that we can reject the null hypothesis of no difference at the 1% level because 2.65 is greater than 2.576. We conclude that mediators are significantly younger than nonmediators.

For the second question the mean number of minutes per spouse-abuse call is 21.4 minutes for "mediators" and 22.12 minutes for "nonmediators." The difference in means is 0.72 minutes and $S_{\bar{x}_1 - \bar{x}_2}$ was found to equal 1.56, $df = 174$. So

$$t = \frac{21.40 - 22.12}{1.56} = \frac{-.72}{1.56} = -.46$$

When we refer to Table 8.4, we find that our obtained t of .46 (ignore the sign) is less in value than the critical t for the 5% level, and conclude that there is not a significant difference in the amount of time spent on spouse-abuse calls for "mediators" and "nonmediators."

The t test is appropriate for testing the significance of the difference between two sample means. If we wish to compare more than two means, we need to use a close relative of the t test, a procedure called analysis of variance ($ANOVA$). This procedure will not be presented here, but it can be found in the suggested readings contained on page 123. Remember that the mean is an appropriate measure of central tendency for interval scaled data, and therefore the t-test and analysis of variance procedures are appropriate for interval scaled data.

CHOOSING A SIGNIFICANCE LEVEL

When testing the significance of χ^2, r, rs, or t, we saw that a decision to reject the null hypothesis depends on the df associated with the test statistic and our choice of level of significance. We noted that the customary levels of significance are the 5% and 1% levels. That is, we reject a null hypothesis if the probability of its being true is less than 5% or 1%. Once again, these significance levels are called $alpha$ (α), and they represent a level of risk that we are willing to assume when we consider an outcome to be $improbable$ when it is, in fact, probable. When we reject a null hypothesis, we are not stating that it is $absolutely$ false, but that it is $probably$ false. When we accept a null hypothesis, we are not contending it is true, but that it is likely to be true.

We noted that alpha defines the probability of a Type-I error. A Type-I error occurs when we falsely reject a true-null hypothesis. In contrast, a Type-II error occurs when a null hypothesis that is actually false is not rejected. While the probability of making a Type-I error is quickly ascertained by noting the significance level used (α), determining the probability of making a Type-II error is more complex.

We are left with a feeling of unease that we could be in error with either decision we make about the null hypothesis (reject or accept). The value of alpha is always greater than zero, so we can always be wrong. Can the risk of error be minimized? Yes. We can minimize a Type-I error by reducing alpha to a lower value, such as 0.01 or 0.0001. Remember that the choice of alpha is arbitrary. Why not play it very safe and reduce alpha to a very low level, say 0.000001? If we did, we would need $extremely$ large values of our test statistics to reject the null hypothesis, and we would sharply increase our likelihood of a Type-II error. As we reduce the probability of committing one type of error, we increase the probability of committing the other. Is this a catch-22 situation? Not totally. We can find a happy medium.

As a rule of thumb, use of the 1% (0.01) alpha level will rarely be criticized. The 5% (0.05) level is also commonly used, but ordinarily no greater risk of Type-I error should be permitted. Should you use 5% or 1%? The answer to this depends to some degree on the "costs" associated with your decision about the null hypothesis. For example, if you are testing the differential effectiveness of a "new" intervention and an "old" intervention, and if the "new" is much more costly to implement, you will probably opt for the more conservative alpha of 1% to minimize the probability of a Type-I error.

Generally speaking, we help to minimize the probability of a Type-II error by exercising good control procedures in our research studies. Whatever we do to reduce sampling error and other sources of error variance will serve to reduce the likelihood of committing a Type-II error. How can we tell when a Type-I or II-error has occurred? We can't. Sometimes we will erroneously retain the null hypothesis when it should have been rejected, and other times we will reject it when it should have been retained. Our happy-medium solution to the problem is to use either the 5% or 1% significance level and do the best we can in controlling extraneous variables in our research endeavors.

Chapter 9

Data Processing

LAWRENCE R. ASKLING

In the previous chapters we have described some of the methods to analyze data and produce descriptive statistics. Data processing is not simply an academic exercise. The purpose of understanding statistics is to provide information to support decisions that are based on the results that are typically presented in some kind of agency or scholarly report. In this chapter we present some very practical steps to enter your data on the computer, to generate statistics, and to produce a report based on the results of your data analysis.

WELCOME TO THE COMPUTER

Data processors (that's you) in most settings use an interactive computer-hardware (machinery) system to enter and run statistical procedures. Interactive means that you are connected to a computer by a keyboard and video-display terminal, and that the computer responds immediately to your directions or commands. In the past, data processors used keypunched cards that could be bent, folded, or mutilated, but cards and keypunch operators are now as common as the Indian-head nickel. You don't have to use a computer, of course, since you have the formulas in this book and can calculate all of the statistics with pencil and paper or hand calculator. This was once a most common (and boring) job of research assistants (RAs). That generation of RAs certainly learned their statistical formulas; however, computer processing is cheaper, faster, and more efficient and accurate.

Colleges, universities, and large and small human-service agencies have computers that have programs or software packages that produce statistical calculations. Three categories of computers are: (1) mainframe computers, (2) minicomputers, and (3) microcomputers.

There are significant and costly differences between these types of computers. Mainframe and minicomputers can manipulate and store large data sets. Large memories are necessary to store both the raw data generated

108

by research instruments and the statistical routines needed to produce statistical calculations. Mainframes and minicomputers have the memory requirements necessary for the most complicated and sophisticated statistics. Microcomputers, on the other hand, have much smaller memories, which limit the size of the raw data set and the type of statistical procedures you will be able to use. Mainframes are used for

> centralized data operations and batch processing . . . but they're expensive and complicated pieces of electronics. [They also require] the elite corps of highly trained, highly paid MIS professionals necessary to keep the mainframes operating properly. . . . Minicomputers . . . although better suited for decentralized and transactional processing, are, nevertheless, only smaller and less expensive versions of the mainframes. . . . They are certainly not simple to use . . . nor can they ever be considered cheap to buy or install (Infoworld, 1984, pp. 65-66).

In recent years microcomputers have become more common in both large and small human-service agencies. Microcomputers fit on the top of a desk, and many are capable of producing the descriptive statistics described in this book by using statistical software programs. Microcomputers have a small memory capacity, which limits the size of the data set (number of cases) that may be used for statistics. The advantage of the microcomputer is that you do not have to be a computer specialist to learn to use the machine; with concentrated practice, microcomputers are also easy to use. Human-service practitioners will not have to rely on data-processing consultants and computer specialists with mainframe credentials to manage data files and produce statistics, but can become skilled in all stages of data analysis. Microcomputers can also be used in conjunction with a mainframe computer or minicomputers. Microcomputers may be used as "dumb" terminals tied into the mainframe or mini, or data may be transferred between the mainframe or mini and the micro. This information may then be analyzed or manipulated by using the mainframe's software.

These three categories of computers are common tools that are used to produce statistical calculations. Two of the most powerful statistical packages available on mainframe and minicomputers are SPSSX and SAS. Several less powerful statistical software packages are available for microcomputers, including a reduced version of SPSS software. The advantages and disadvantages of computer-data processing include:

1. Computer processing reduces the amount of time required to calculate statistics. Computers are fast. This means that we may obtain statistical results within minutes or hours rather than days or weeks. (According to Grinnell (1981, p. 532) the computer "allows investigators to expand their analysis of data beyond small sample sizes and simple research designs. Without a computer, it is difficult to work with sample sizes larger than 25 and to apply statistical techniques to them by hand."
2. Computers produce statistics with a high degree of accuracy. Researchers trust the numbers produced by computers. If an error occurs, it is

most likely the result of faulty-data entry, one of the most serious threats to producing valid results. Data-entry problems will be dealt with later.

3. With some practice, computers are easy to use. Computer-software programs for the social sciences allow even the beginner to produce complex statistics. This is also a disadvantage since novices may use inappropriate statistics because they do not understand the assumptions or theory behind a statistical procedure or test. "In short, computers may often expand investigators' skills beyond their statistical understanding, so that they attempt more than they should" (Grinnell, 1981, p. 532).

4. Computers are dumb machines. Kerlinger (1973) calls them stupid. They may be fast and efficient, but you have to tell computers what to do. Just as you drive a car, you direct the computer. In data processing you are in charge of organizing the data, entering the data, selecting statistical procedures, and interpreting the statistics. Once you understand and appreciate this basic fact, it is easy to develop a meaningful, working relationship with the computer. The selection of the appropriate statistical procedures depends, of course, on your understanding of the statistics presented in this book, rather than on your understanding of the computer.

Computers are an important tool in the social work decision-making process. However, many practitioners are afraid of the computer and suffer from chipophobia. Contrary to the statements of computer advertisers, computer processing does take time to learn. There is more involved in operating a computer than in turning on a television set. Computer centers typically offer free short courses to help you learn to use the computer for data and statistical processing. Computer consultants are usually available to help you with technical, but not logical, problems. With a minimum of computer skills you should be able to produce the statistics described in this book. All that is required to begin using a computer is a minimum of typing skills and some determination.

Data processors develop their own methods and shortcuts for analyzing data. The following steps may be a helpful guide to data analysis: (1) organizing raw data, (2) entering the raw data on the computer terminal, (3) checking your data entry for errors, (4) selecting statistical procedures, (5) analyzing your data, and (6) interpreting data.

AID TO FAMILIES WITH DEPENDENT CHILDREN (ADC) STUDY

We use a data set from a social-welfare policy study to illustrate these data analysis procedures. In October 1981, the Reagan Administration implemented changes in the eligibility requirements of the ADC program. Part of a strategy to reduce social welfare spending, the Omnibus Reconciliation Act of 1981 (OBRA) rule changes resulted in the removal of more than four thousand families from the ADC program in a midwestern state. A research project was undertaken to study the economic, social, and health affects on families removed from the program. The study was conducted 15 months after ADC recipients were cut from the program.

ADC is one of the most controversial welfare programs. Its purpose is to protect children whose parents have little or no income. Cash payments and medical assistance (Medicaid) are provided by ADC to families headed by single parents, predominantly women, or to families with two parents if one is incapacitated or if both parents are unemployed. Most of those cuts from the program had incomes that exceeded 150 percent of the state standard of need (adjusted by family size).

A condensed research interview instrument is presented in Appendix B. The structured interviews were conducted by telephone, and the instrument was used to structure the interview. The questions on the instrument were closed-ended (yes/no, multiple choice) or open-ended (respondents provided answer). The interviews on the average were about 45 minutes long. A portion of the data set developed from these interviews is presented in Appendix B. We refer to both the instrument and the data set throughout this discussion.

ORGANIZING RAW DATA: STEP 1

Regardless of what computer system you are using, you will need to organize the raw data. Each data-collection instrument (questionnaire, interview schedule) is a single case (called a record). An instrument consists of questions (variables) and answers or responses (values). For computer processing the answers/values must be recorded as numeric values. The process of transforming the answers from an instrument to a numeric value is called coding. The major goal of coding is interpretability. There must be some order to your coding so that others can make sense of what you have done. If others may use the data set you are working on, you should provide instructions about how you coded the data. Depending on the complexity of a study, coding may be done directly from the research instrument or transferred to a coding sheet. Coding sheets (see Appendix C) often help organize long research instruments.

Data are entered on the computer line by line. Each line is eighty or fewer columns wide (exceptions certainly exist, but for practical purposes and for SPSSX users, one line of data is limited to 80 or fewer columns). However, when using a video display terminal, we prefer to limit the columns to 69 to prevent the terminal from wrapping around (seemingly moving to the next line although the line number remains the same). Wraparounds are visually disconcerting, particularly if you use previous data for column guides. As you organize your data and assign numeric values to the categories of your variables, one or more columns (for one or more digits) on the computer terminal are associated with each variable. For each case a variable should have one value. Depending on the question/variable (hereafter called variable), you assign a number for each different value.

In another chapter we presented one of the most important equations in social-science research, $Gi = Go$. This formula is equivalent in importance to Einstein's theory of relativity and simply means "Garbage in equals garbage out." We repeat this concept because we cannot overemphasize the importance of a well-designed methodology and instrument. Computer processing has the awesome power to appear to make bad data look good. There is an elegance associated with transforming data from the instrument to digits displayed across a computer terminal. These digits seem to become more real than the respondents' replies. Computer processing is *not proof* that the data are worth the effort. Computer processing can hide serious flaws in the design of a research or evaluation instrument. A well-designed study is the most important step to producing valid conclusions.

KINDS OF VARIABLES

Many scales exist for gathering social-science information. Typical kinds of questions include: true and false, multiple choice, agree-disagree attitude questions, rank-order questions, semantic differential, and open-ended questions. There are many texts, handbooks, and guides that describe the development and use of indexes and scales (Grinnell, 1981, Chap. 8, pp. 130-155), and these should be referred to for detailed information. In this chapter, we are only concerned with working with the information from the instrument, rather than with designing the instrument.

There are certain conventions that are useful to follow when coding data. Each variable or item on an instrument must be assigned a variable name. If you use SPSSX for your statistical processing, select a name that has eight or fewer characters, the first being a letter. A helpful hint is to choose names that are associated with the question. For example, "A1" might be the first-attitude question or "SEX" might refer to the subject's gender. Avoid complex data names containing hieroglyphic combinations of letters and numerals such as CB1XSIP (Citizen Broadcasting News Service in Panama). Such combinations may be meaningful to you when you write the name, but they are a nuisance to remember and they invite typing errors when manipulating data or requesting statistical procedures. Keep names simple!

After specifying a variable name, you must decide all of the possible values that an answer may require. The values may be the actual numeric answer, such as for age, height, weight, income, amount of ADC check, and hours worked per week. Values may have no numeric or "real" meaning at all. Values may be meaningful only to the extent that they are associated with one and only one answer and have no numeric relationship to other values. The following section describes some conventions by which six common kinds of research questions are coded.

1. True/false questions require two steps to code. If you have asked fact or knowledge questions with a correct answer, first determine whether

the reply is correct or wrong. Code correct answers as "1" and wrong answers as "0." This convention permits you to combine T/F variables and to determine the total number of correct numbers. The frequency count also reports the total number of correct replies. Attitude type of true/false questions may be handled as yes/no questions described next.

2. Many surveys ask questions that are answered with "yes" or "no." We code no as "0" and yes as "1." This convention is useful if you choose to combine yes/no variables into one scaled index.

   We used several yes/no questions in the ADC study. For example we asked, "When you were growing up, did your family ever receive ADC benefits?" "Yes" replies were coded as "1" and "no" replies as "0." This convention was maintained consistently throughout the study. This convention is also maintained by the University of Iowa School of Social Work Research Center for other studies, so that we do not have to spend time trying to decipher a researcher's coding scheme.

3. Multiple-choice items are often used on surveys. There are three conventional ways to code multiple-choice questions, depending on the type of question. Respondents have a choice of (1) choosing one response, (2) choosing one or more responses, or (3) selecting the right answers. The kind of question determines how you code the data. When only one choice is to be made, you would code the participants' selection, typically 1 through 5 (if there are five choices). If multiple responses are possible, you usually treat each possible answer as a separate variable with a value like that of a yes/no question. You then code "1," which means that "respondent chose this answer," or "0," which means that "respondent did not chose this answer." When a multiple-choice item has right and wrong answers you will code the right answer as "1" and the wrong answer as "0," similar to the T/F situation.

   Several multiple-choice questions were used in the ADC study. We asked, "Think back to the time when you were cut from ADC. How serious did you think it would be? Did it present an extremely serious problem for you, a somewhat serious problem, or was it not a serious problem for you?" Respondents had a choice of three answers. *Extremely serious* was coded a "1," *somewhat serious* as "2," and *not serious* as "3."

4. Attitude items, where respondents express an attitude or opinion like "Social work research is a must!" are frequently used on instruments. These items are often characterized by "strongly agree" to "strongly disagree," "positive to negative," and "liberal to conservative" continuums. Attitude scales frequently range from 1 to 7, 1 to 9, 1 to 4, 1 to 6, or 1 to 5. Code the items from right to left, from 1 to the appropriate last digit. Attitude items, though theoretically considered to be ordinal level items, are usually handled as interval-level data. However, well constructed attitude-type scales frequently reverse the positive and

negative polarities of the scales: attitude items may have positive or negative implications or the agree to disagree (positive to negative) continuums are reversed for each question. This requires recoding of appropriate questions so that the positive or "most strongly agree" end of the scale is consistent for all variables. In other words, 1 should either mean "strongly agree" (positive) or "strongly disagree" (negative), but it should not mean both.

5. Many variables have real values. For example, you may code a respondent's actual age, height, weight, income, etc. Simply code the numbers directly as given by the respondent. There are times when you may want to reduce the number of categories for the variables, but that can be done by recoding the data. Do not throw away useful raw data even though you anticipate recoding your data. You may decide to run a test requiring a higher level of data.

Many questions in the ADC study solicited actual or real values. For example, we asked ADC parent's age, education, total income before and after cut, total expenses before and after cut, child-care payments, and frequency for going to a physician. We were able to confirm much of these data with Department of Human Service records, but usually we had to trust that respondents were not lying about their age or income.

6. Open-ended questions are often asked on instruments. However, the analyses you can do with them are limited because of the nature of such questions. Each reply requires a different numerical value or category. Create a list of categories (values) based on respondents' replies, using a simple form of content analysis that places the reply in the best fitting or most descriptive category. When many responses are made with very little repetition, it is often easier to do the analysis by hand, since you can do little more than report frequency counts. However, if the responses are fairly limited and you have many respondents, you may find it useful to code open-ended questions for the computer. Each unique response should be assigned a value.

The ADC data have many open-ended questions. For example, the question, "If you would like to see some changes in your life, what would they be?" had 13 unique responses. *Education* was coded as "01," *more money* as "02," etc.

A "Code Book" is a helpful guide for organizing raw data. A "Code Book" should be developed when other researchers will use the data set you have organized. The Coding Organization Form presented in Appendix C is one guide that may be used to organize your code book. In column one write the variable number from the survey instrument. In column two write the variable name. The columns needed to record raw data should be listed in column three. Column four is used to describe the level of measurement for a variable. Chapter 2 describes the nominal, ordinal, and interval levels. Use of this column helps you select the appropriate statistics. In column five write the possible values with the specific answers or list the range of possible values. Once you have determined the range of values for one variable, such as 1 to 2, 1 to 20, 1 to 99, or 1 to 999, etc., you may assign one or more columns that are needed to store the values on the computer.

The Coding Organization Form used for the ADC study is presented in Appendix B. This sample ADC data set contains 50 cases (interviews with 50 ADC mothers), 101 variables based on questions from those interviews, and requires three lines on the computer terminal for data entry. Display B2 of Appendix B reproduces the Code Book for the ADC study, using the "Coding Organization Form." The first column in that form identifies the question number on the instrument associated with a variable. The second column lists the variable name selected from the survey instrument. The names relate to the survey question. For example, MAGE means ADC mother's age. The third column lists the columns on the video-display terminal that are used to store the variable's values. MAGE requires 2 columns to record the data; thus in the third column we show that MAGE occupies columns 1 and 2 on line 1 of our computer-data file. The fourth column lists the measurement level of the variable (nominal to interval) and can be used as a guide in selecting statistical procedures. For example, MAGE is an interval-level variable because age is measured in years. The fifth column lists either all possible values and their meaning or a range of values. The range of values for MAGE is 18 to 99. The second variable is education, its variable name is ED. ED has a range from 00 to 99, although we expect actual values to be from 6 (coded as 06) elementary to masters 16 (16) or doctorate 18 (18) degrees. ED is an interval-level item, since it is measured in years. ED requires two columns to record the data, and since it follows MAGE, it occupies columns 3 and 4. When a variable has a value that needs two or more columns, be sure to adjust the least values. For example, if an ADC parent's education level is 6, then enter "06" on the computer. If you enter "6" the value would equal "60." You may enter "6," but we find it easier to use the zero instead of the blank, since we prefer to use blanks as missing values. This procedure continues until you fill the desired number of columns.

In the ADC example the first line is arbitrarily limited to 65 columns to avoid the wraparound on the video-display terminal. The last variable entered on that line is REDUCE. The first variable of line 2 is CCNOW (Are your children receiving child care?) and the last variable on line 2 is LIFE (Is your life situation today better, the same, or worse than when you were cut from ADC?). Line 2 has 49 columns, Line 3 begins with EV1 (First Event—Has someone in your family needed emergency medical care in the last year, yes or no?). The last variable is RELATE (How do you feel about your relationship to your children? Would you say things are good, could be better, or there is a lot of tension?). Line 3 has 37 columns.

There are other ways to organize your raw data. Many people simply use a blank survey form and write the variable name next to the question, assign numeric values to the possible answers for each question, and write the columns that are used for data entry on the computer under the variable name.

However, for novice researchers the form used here forces you to select the level of your data for each variable, something you must understand when involved in statistical analysis. We suggest you use this form for complicated coding schemes (and use the form as a reference) or until you thoroughly understand levels of measurement, and you do not have to stop to think what nominal, ordinal, or interval means.

You are ready to begin entering the data on the computer. Since we have 50 cases and three lines of data per case, we have 150 lines in the data file. You have a choice of entering the data directly from the instrument or using a coding sheet. A coding sheet looks like graph paper except that they are eighty columns wide and 24 rows deep. A coding sheet is most helpful when each case requires several lines of data, or the research instrument is so complicated, it would be best to transfer the values to a sheet from which you can then type directly. A coding sheet sometimes helps you locate typing errors, assuming the values you wrote on the coding sheet are accurate. The way the information appears on the coding sheet is the way it should appear on the computer terminal.

One other helpful hint for coding data. Two variables that may help in the processing of data are case and line numbers. Some researchers do not like to assign a value for each case, but the use of this variable sometimes helps to locate errors or find unusual cases. When each case contains several lines of data, we sometimes use line numbers (1, 2, 3, 4, etc.) to help keep track of the data. Line numbers tell you if you skipped a line or help you find errors.

ENTERING DATA ON THE COMPUTER: STEP 2

Once you have coded the data the way you want to enter it on the computer, you are ready to implement step two. Entering data requires that you be familiar with the interactive text editor or word-processing system available with your computer. Interactive means that you use a terminal (keyboard and video-display terminal (VDT)) to communicate with the computer. Text editors enter information line by line and have associated line (row) and column numbers that help manage the data file. Word-processing systems are generally more flexible for data entry and editing. However, they may not be able to manipulate columns as well as text editors. Since the decline of punch cards, text editors have been the dominant way to enter data on mainframe computers. However, word-processing programs are becoming increasingly available on mainframes and will probably replace text editors for most purposes. On microcomputers, data entry is usually done using word-processing software. You must become familiar with the text editor or word-processing system to enter data. That information is available through your computing center or software manuals (if you are using a micrcomputer). Most interactive systems are simple to use for basic data entry and, with experience, are very powerful systems for manipulating raw data.

Through the text editing or word-processing system, you can enter the data, check and correct errors, run the statistical procedures you want, revise and update the data, and store the data set for future reference. Your data are stored in a long-term memory, which is usually called a file. That file is stored on a disk or magnetic tape referred to as a library.

After you have entered your raw data, you need to write instructions for obtaining the statistical analysis of your data. The ADC raw data is presented in Appendix B. You must select one of the common statistical packages that are available for your computer system. SPSSX and SAS are two of the most common packages that provide the statistical analyses used in this book. Other statistical programs are available for mainframes, minicomputers, or microcomputers. Once again you have some additional homework to do. Statistical packages like SPSSX or SAS require instructions to process data. You must tell SPSSX and SAS what the variables are and what columns they occupy in the raw data file. You may take this information from your coding form. You can also help yourself read and interpret the computer output if you choose optional instructions that produce more descriptive variable names or assign names (when appropriate) to categorical values.

MISSING VALUES

One of the most vexing problems in social work research is missing values. What do you do when a respondent fails to reply to your questions? You must decide what to do with missing values because they affect your statistics, particularly if you create new variables or examine relationships between variables. A case is usually excluded from statistical analysis when a missing value is encountered for the variable(s) you are analyzing. Statistical packages allow you to assign a blank or other number (a convention is "99" or "999"). A convention for entering missing data on the raw-data file is to type a "blank" or "space" in the associated column or columns. There are times when you may want to replace missing values with a mean or median value and many statistical programs allow you to do this as part of a statistical procedure. If not, you must change the value in the raw data.

CHECKING FOR RAW DATA ERRORS: STEP 3

Next, you must check the raw data for errors. The major source of errors in statistical processing with the computer is typos you make by typing the wrong number. These are sometimes extremely difficult to locate without careful search. The major method for tracing errors is to run a frequency count for all variables. You can check the range and values to determine if an error exists. This simple step is often omitted and can result in embarrassing errors and a need to reanalyze your data. The next most common source of error is that the column description for your variables does not match the raw data.

A second method of checking for errors is to list raw data on a printout or to do a LIST procedure that lists the values of each variable for each case. Both SPSSX and SAS contain list procedures.

Once you have checked and rechecked your data for data-entry errors, you may then begin the data analysis.

SELECTING STATISTICAL PROCEDURES: STEP 4

First obtain a valid frequency count. Frequency data can show the count for each value, percents, data range, and some basic descriptive statistics such as mean and standard deviation. Further analysis depends on your developing an understanding of your variables. Some researchers call this "wallowing" in your data. We do not think it can be stressed often enough how important it is to understand how your individual variables are distributed. Which are nominal, ordinal, or interval? The statistical procedures you use are based on this elementary knowledge. An error that novices often make is that they want to examine relationships between variables (sometimes in search of an elusive significance) without bothering to "wallow" in the frequency data. Without a thorough understanding of individual variables, novices proceed to examine relationships between variables. The end result not only is frustration, but also a high probability of missing significant relationships. This book has been designed to help you select the procedures and then interpret the statistical results. Data analysis should proceed from the simple to the complex, especially if you are new to research. Understand your frequency counts and percents. Understand what the means and medians imply for interval data. Understand how individual variables are distributed before investigating how variables are jointly distributed.

MODIFYING VARIABLES

At this point you may create new variables by combining (adding, subtracting, multiplying, or dividing) existing variables, or you may want to change the values of existing variables. Most statistical packages on the computer allow you to change a variable's value without modifying the raw-data file. In SPSSX you may use the RECODE, COMPUTE, COUNT, and IF commands. RECODE lets you reduce the number of categories (range of values) or change an old value to a new value. The COMPUTE command creates a new variable as some combination of one or more existing variables. The COUNT command is a variation of the COMPUTE command and simply counts the number of times a respondent gave the same answer (e.g., "Yes" or "Agree") to more than one item (variables). The IF command allows you to create a new variable based on one or more conditions of a variable. You may want to combine related variables to produce a scaled variable. In social work research many self-esteem type scales are created from a list or set of variables. You do not need to fully understand how these commands are used. The associated statistical manuals can help do that, but you should be aware that raw data may be changed in a variety of ways to assist with your statistical analysis.

We created several computed variables with the ADC data set. One such computed variable was called EVENTS. In the ADC study we asked the families about the kinds of problems their family experienced within the last year. We simply count the problems checked to produce the new variable that contains the number of problems reported by the respondent. This manipulation does not take into account that certain problems may be more serious than others.

APPROACHING DATA ANALYSIS: STEP 5

What are the boundaries of your data analysis? How many relationships should you examine? Your data analysis should seek to answer your research questions or hypotheses. We have adapted Glaser's and Strauss' distinctions between "logico-deductive" and "grounded-theory" approaches to theory verification and generation to apply to decisions required by data analysis.

There are two approaches to data analysis: logico-deductive and grounded-theory. The logico-deductive approach is used to verify sociological and psychological theories. The grounded-theory approach is used to generate theories from the data (Glaser and Strauss, 1967). Whichever approach you use will affect the data analysis, but the grounded-theory approach is typically used (in practice if not theory) in social work.

With logico-deductive approach, you examine only the relationships that specifically concern your hypotheses. You limit your examination of data to testing your theories and hypotheses. This approach provides useful boundaries to your investigation. You are less likely to be overwhelmed with masses of data that may not only confuse, but also which you may never use. Strict theoreticians expect that you adhere to this approach.

The grounded-theory approach to data analysis is concerned with the "discovery of theory from data systematically obtained from social research" (Glaser and Strauss, 1967, p. 2). Rather than test a theory, you investigate research questions without having a preconceived idea or hypothesis about the results. In this approach you examine several or all possible relationships. Instead of using a rod and reel to fish, you use a net stretched the width and depth of the river. You may not only catch the trout, but also you are quite likely to land carp. These fishing expeditions are common, given the ease of computer processing. The grounded-theory approach is often used to generate information that may be used in the decision-making process in a human-service agency.

Treasure hunts without a map sometimes prove seductive. Why not try to test all relationships? Are there other statistical procedures that may be used? There is not enough space available in the Library of Congress to store all of the books if the results for every variable and all possible relationships were produced. Sooner or later you will have to decide that enough is enough. The better you "wallow" in your data, the more informed you are when you choose to end your data analysis.

By the time you reach the end of your data analysis, you may have several inches of computer printouts stacked in front of you. Your work is just beginning, but the risk of data burnout is high. You have put hours on hours into data entry and running statistics. Now you are at the stage when you have to do something with all of those data; you have to provide order to the chaos. You must interpret the results. You must translate the numbers back into words, sentences, and paragraphs. Select the variables and relationships you want to discuss. These variables and relationships should have been selected, based on your research questions, hypotheses, ideas, or formal theories that were used in developing the study in the first place.

You can interpret the findings from the computer printouts. Write on the printouts, the paper will soon disintegrate. There is nothing sacred about clean, computer printouts: use them as worksheets that help you wallow in the data—draw lines, circles, or arrows to help make sense of the chaos. But always give clean printouts to faculty or your agency director; they like to doodle too. Write your interpretations next to the table. Separate the printout pages and arrange them in the order that you want to describe the data. Leave the computer and begin interpreting the data. Sit at a typewriter or word processor and interpret the results. With experience you may even write your report on the computer, as we did this book. Are your results the same or different from findings and conclusions presented by other researchers? How do your findings relate to the literature? What can you conclude from all that work you have just done? Did you answer the questions you wanted to learn about when you first designed the study? Did you answer other questions that developed as you devoted more and more time to the project?

WRITING THE REPORT: STEP 6

There are many guides to writing research reports. If your report is being prepared for an agency, then your agency may have guidelines for you to follow. In university settings, a fairly standard model is used. The organization of the research report includes (1) literature review and problem definition, (2) method used to gather data, (3) findings of your data analysis, and (4) discussion and conclusions (Grinnell, 1981, p. 556).

Problem definition describes the purpose of your study. This section generally contains a review of the literature. From that review you have provided the reader with an understanding about the ideas, hypotheses, and theories that researchers have about your topic. This section is used to describe your hypotheses or research questions that may be the same or different from the literature. This section is used to describe your definition of the key variables in the study.

The method section simply describes how you gathered your data. You should describe how you selected your sample or population, developed instruments (surveys, etc.), and collected your data. This description should be thorough so that another researcher can redo your study (replicate) using your procedures. The validity of your findings often depends on a clear description of your method.

Most of this book has been oriented to assist you in writing findings for descriptive studies. The findings section presents the results of the study and the tables and graphs that are used to illustrate the data. Tables and graphs are extremely useful as a tool to help present results.

The discussion section integrates your findings with your problem-definition section. How are your results different from those of the literature? The discussion section goes beyond a basic description of the results presented in the findings section. The discussion section is used to interpret those findings. The discussion includes implications for theory or practice or recommends policy changes. The discussion section is your last and best opportunity to communicate your ideas. A discussion section begins and ends with a brief summary statement that reviews the important findings of your study. This is your last opportunity to get in the last word. And this is our last word: Good luck with your research.

References and Suggested Readings

Babbie, E. R. (1983). *The practice of social research* (3rd ed.). Belmont, CA: Wadsworth.

Bailey, K. D. (1982). *Methods of social research* (2nd ed.). New York: Free Press.

Blalock, H. M., Jr. (1979). *Social statistics* (Rev. 2nd ed.). New York: McGraw-Hill.

Glaser, B. G., & Strauss, A. L. (1967). *The discovery of grounded theory: Strategies for qualitative research.* New York: Aldine.

Grinnell, R. M., Jr. (1985). *Social work research and evaluation. 2nd ed.* Itasca, IL: F. E. Peacock Publishers.

Guilford, J. P. (1950). *Fundamental statistics in psychology and education* (2nd ed.). New York: McGraw-Hill.

Katzer, J., Cook, K. H., & Crouch, W. W. (1978). *Evaluating information: A guide for users of social science research.* Reading, MA: Addison-Wesley.

Kerlinger, F. N. (1973). *Foundations of behavioral research* (2nd ed.). New York: Holt, Rinehart and Winston.

SAS. (1982). *SAS user's guide: Basics 1982 edition.* Cary, NC: SAS Institute.

Selltiz, C., Wrightsman, L. S., & Cook, S. W. (1976). *Research methods in social relations* (2nd ed.). New York: Holt, Rinehart and Winston.

Siegel, S. (1956). *Nonparametric statistics: For the behavioral sciences.* New York: McGraw-Hill.

Special report: Micros, mainframes and you, the user (1984, April 7). *Infoworld, 6*(19), pp. 65-66.

Spence, J. T., Cotton, J. W., Underwood, W. J., & Duncan, C. P. (1983). *Elementary statistics* (4th ed.). Englewood Cliffs: Prentice-Hall.

SPSSX. (1983). *SPSSX user's guide.* New York: McGraw-Hill.

Stahl, S. M., & Hennes, J. D. (1980). *Reading and understanding applied statistics* (2nd ed.). St. Louis: C.V. Mosby.

APPENDIX A

POLICE PERCEPTIONS STUDY

This appendix contains the data collection instrument, raw data, and variable coding sheets from a study of police attitudes and practices in domestic disturbance cases. The study was carried out by Marcia L. Traylor as a M.S.W. Thesis, under the supervision of the author of this book.

The questionnaire and data used here are a reduced version of the original instrument and data.

Nearly 500 questionnaires were sent to chiefs of police in five Iowa cities. The chiefs had agreed to distribute the instruments to their officers and collect and return completed ones. One-hundred-ninety-four questionnaires were returned, for an overall response rate of 40%. The revised questionnaire is presented here as Display A1.

The returned questionnaires were identified and coded according to the schema shown in Display A2. Note in Display A2 that each variable is assigned a number, a name, data column(s), category code values, and a level of measurement. This type of coding format is (was) used to create the raw data, matrix shown in Display A3, and to aid in programming the computer for data processing and statistical analysis.

Display A3 contains the data from 194 respondents for the 60 variables shown in Display A2. Data entry for these 60 variables requires 66 data columns, since several variables require two-digit codes.

Display A4 shows a basic SPSSX program of instructions that serves to input and identify the variables and their corresponding data. Additional instructions are necessary to provide for specific analyses, such as CROSSTABS and SCATTERGRAMS.

Adequate information is provided in Displays A1–A4 for you to do a partial or complete descriptive analysis and presentation of the data generated in this study. Specific research questions to be asked and answered are left to the discretion of the student(s) and course instructors. We recommend that several different types of analyses be completed, the results presented in tables and graphs, and a brief report of the findings and conclusions be written and shared. One becomes proficient at doing by doing.

DISPLAY A1

<u>POLICE PERCEPTIONS ON SPOUSE ABUSE AND DOMESTIC VIOLENCE</u>

The majority of this survey concerns various aspects of spouse abuse, such as degree of violence, presence of a weapon, living arangements of the two partners, evidence of the use of alcohol, legal alternatives available, police involvement, and rates of incidence of spouse abuse. The purpose of this survey is to gather only your <u>perceptions</u> concerning these factors of spouse abuse. You are not expected to know the actual statistics to answer the questions. Just make your best guess on each question.

<u>Section 1 Personal and Family Background</u>

1. Age (in years) _____

2. Marital Status: Married _____ Single _____ Divorced _____
   Widowed _____

3. Sex: Male _____ Female _____

4. Number of years in law enforcement? _____

5. Number of years on present police force? _____

6. Your father's education (check one): High School _____ Voc.
   Tech. _____ 1-4 years college _____ 4-year degree _____
   Professional degree _____

7. Do you feel that you came from a family that experienced spouse
   abuse? Yes _____ No _____

Section II

Use these percents to answer questions 8-10:

1	2	3	4	5	6
0-15%	15-25%	25-40%	40-55%	55-70%	70%-over

8. In what percent of the calls you respond to are the partners married? _____

9. What percent of all spouse-abuse incidences are responded to by the police? _____

10. What percent of spouse calls are repeat calls? _____

11. Do you feel there has been an increase in spouse abuse in your area during the past 5-10 years?

    Yes _____   No _____

12. Do you feel that legal punishment deters further abuse?

    Yes _____   No _____

    What is the most frequent advice you give to the victim when you respond to a call?

13. _____ Contact a social service agency

14. _____ File a complaint

15. _____ Press charges

16. _____ Move out

17. _____ Leave temporarily

18. _____ Seek counseling and/or advice from friends, relatives, etc.

19. _____ Seek an injuction

    Other: _____

20. Do you feel that injuctions are effective?

       Yes _____   No _____

What role do you take in spouse-abuse calls?

21. Mediator   _____

22. Counselor   _____

23. Only there to break them apart   _____

24. Advisor for both parties   _____

Other: _____

25. Can you arrest the abuser even if the victim does not intend to
press charges?

       Yes _____   No _____

26. How often do you make this type of arrest?

      Rarely (less than 10% of the time)   _____

      Sometimes (10% to 50% of the time)   _____

      Frequently (more than 50% of the time) _____

27. Do you feel crisis intervention teams are a good idea?

       Yes _____   No _____

28. Do you think they are a better way to handle domestic violence
than the way your department deals with family disturbances now?

       Yes _____   No _____

29. If it was feasible, would you be willing to have a social worker
accompany you to domestic disturbance calls?

       Yes _____   No _____

30. How much difference is there between what you are taught at the
police academy and the policies your department follows?
Rate this on the scale of 1 to 5

                        1   2   3   4   5

Hardly any   A big

difference   différence

31. Do you feel that there are times when you find yourself having to

    take on the role of counselor or social worker?

              Yes _____   No _____

32. Does taking this role mean spending more time with the parties

    involved than you normaly would?

              Yes _____   No _____

33. Do you feel there is any distinction between spouse abuse in the

    home and assault on the streets?

              Yes _____   No _____

    If yes, is your feeling based on (check one):

34. knowledge of the law regarding spouse abuse   _____

35. general public opinion   _____

36. personal experience   _____

37. the idea that the types of violence   _____

      are different

38. If the abuse is perpetrated without the use of a weapon but

    includes physical assault, how long do you think a woman

    typically waits to summon help from the police?

         1 month _____   6 months _____

         1 to 2 years _____   over 3 years _____

39. Given the same abuse circumstances as above, how long do you

    think a woman waits to summon help from other social agencies?

         1 month _____   6 months _____

1 to 2 years _____   over 3 years _____

40. How long do you think a woman typically waits to press charges:

    After first call   _____

    After second call   _____

    After third call   _____

    When she has obtained

    an injuction   _____

    She doesn't usually

    press any charges   _____

41. Do you think there is a correlation between how severely a woman
    was abused and whether or not she pressed charges?

                Yes _____   No _____

42. What percent of male partners involved with spouse abuse do you
    feel were <u>drinking</u> at the time of the abuse? (circle one)

        1   2   3   4   5   6

     0-15%   15-25%   25-40%   40-55%   55-70%   70%-over

43. What percent of the male partners involved with spouse abuse do
    you feel were <u>drunk</u> at the time of the abuse?

       _____ (use same percents as above)

44. How much of an influence do you think alcohol is in spouse-abuse
    cases? (circle one)

    Rank in order of influence: 1 being low and 10 being high

        1   2   3   4   5   6   7   8   9   10

For the next five statements (items 45-49), rank each as to whether you agree or disagree on a scale of 1 to 7 with 1 being strongly agree and 7 being strongly disagree.

45. Even if the couple is separated for awhile, the woman usually returns home to the man. _____

46. Abusive men usually regret their actions and reform even if the abuse has been going on for a long time. _____

47. There are more women seeking divorces from abusive men now than there were 10 years ago. _____

48. Most men are abusive only during one relationship with a particular woman. _____

49. When they are separated from a particular woman, most men stop being abusive. _____

50. Blank item, not used in this book

51. Rate how you think the public supports your department's policy on how officers should respond to domestic violence calls.

    1 = does not support;   10 = fully supports

      1   2   3   4   5   6   7   8   9   10

Section III

52. Estimate the length of time you spend on each spouse-abuse call in minutes. _____

53. Do you usually handle spouse-abuse calls alone (that is, at least 50% of the time)?

              Yes _____   No _____

54. If yes, are you comfortable with this arrangement?

              Yes _____   No _____

55. Do you feel there is a need for more extensive training in the area of domestic violence?

        Yes _____   No _____

56. Would you spend time in a workshop or class to get further training in this area?

        Yes _____   No _____

57. Do you think that the training you get now is sufficient for you to handle spouse-abuse calls effectively?

        Yes _____   No _____

58. Instead of taking a workshop or class later on, should the initial training be lengthened to include more material on domestic violence?

        Yes _____   No _____

59. Do you feel there is a need for a spouse-abuse shelter in your area?

        Yes _____   No _____

Comments:

60. City _____

DISPLAY A2

Coding Organization Form
Police Perceptions Study

Variable No.	Variable Name	Data In Column(s)	Measurement Level	Category Codes
1	AGE	1-2	I	---
2	MARSTAT	3	N	1=Married 2=Single 3=Divorced 4=Widowed
3	SEX	4	N	1=Male 2=Female
4	YRSLAWEN	5-6	I	
5	YRSPOLIC	7-8	I	
6	FATHEDUC	9	O	1=HS, 2=VOC., 3=1-4 college 4=4-year Degree 5=Prof Degree
7	CAMEFROM	10	N	1=Yes 2=No
8	PARTMAR	11	O	1 to 6
9	POLRESPD	12	O	1 to 6
10	REPEAT	13	O	1 to 6
11	INCREASE	14	N	1=Yes 2=No
12	PUNDETER	15	N	1=Yes 2=No
13	SSA	16	N	1=Check 2=No Check
14	FILECOMP	17	N	1=
15	PRESCHAR	18	N	1=
16	MOVEOUT	19	N	1=
17	LEVTEMP	20	N	1=
18	FRIENDS	21	N	1=
19	INJUNC	22	N	1=Check 2=No Check
20	INJEFFEC	23	N	1=Yes 2=No
21	MEDIATOR	24	N	1=Check 2=No Check
22	COUNCEL	25	N	1=
23	BREKAPAR	26	N	1=
24	BOTHPART	27	N	1=Check 2=No Check
25	ARREST	28	N	1=Yes 2=No
26	OFTARRES	29	O	1 to 3
27	TEAMS	30	N	1=Yes 2=No
28	BETTERWA	31	N	1=Yes 2=No
29	SWACCOMP	32	N	1=Yes 2=No
30	DIFFEREN	33	O	1 to 5
31	DOSOWORK	34	N	1=Yes 2=No
32	MORETIME	35	N	1=Yes 2=No
33	DISTINCT	36	N	1=Yes 2=No
34	KNOWLAW	37	N	1=Check 2=No Check
35	PUBOPIN	38	N	1=Check 2=No Check
36	PEREXDER	39	N	1=Check 2=No Check
37	TYPEDIFF	40	N	1=Check 2=No Check
38	NOWEAPON	41	O	1 to 4
39	WOWAITS	42	O	1 to 4

40	WOPRECHAR	43	N	1 to 5
41	CORRABOS	44	N	1=Yes 2=No
42	DRINKING	45	O	1 to 6
43	DRUNK	46	O	1 to 6
44	INFLU	47-48	O	1 to 10
45	RETURNS	49	O	1 to 7
46	REGRET	50	O	1 to 7
47	DIVORCES	51	O	1 to 7
48	ONERELA	52	O	1 to 7
49	SEPSTOP	5	O	1 to 7
49	PUBSUPP	54	O	1 to 7
51	RANKSUPP	55-56	O	1 to 10
52	LENGMIN	57-58	I	0 to ?
53	ALONE	59	N	1=Yes 2=No
54	COMFORT	60	N	1=Yes 2=No
55	NEEDTRAI	61	N	1=Yes 2=No
56	WORKSHOP	62	N	1=Yes 2=No
57	TRNSUFF	63	N	1=Yes 2=No
58	TRNLENG	64	N	1=Yes 2=No
59	SHELTER	65	N	1=Yes 2=No
60	CITY	66	N	1 to 5

DISPLAY A3

```
25110403124 3 122221222221221222111122122 516610343331   302 221211
29120807525251222221222221211222122122121 2516510262651  102 221211
27110505116251122221222122222111241122222423 16509472 71  202 111111
23210101426361222221221122221211412222222213144075326620 32021112111
2121      324 32 22221122221211112311122211231550854542207202 112211
27110606325441122211222221121222511122211252 6610170371  1522221111
43111010121 31222212222222111121411 12221  51530827165209202 112111
38111414 15 6222222122222121  211122222  52651071   1   102 12  11
30110707114661211121122112222111251112221333 26610171772 01302 112111
2721080142 351222212222221212222 11222213452550615747210  22221211
26110505126161222122222221221122 5222      16610151771  0211121211
28120707124652111111122111121 223112    1516510272561  152 111221
38111111125 31222122222122111112 122    1152641067346206102 22 211
28110606224351122112222122222222231112211  51660916124205302 112111
43111515124441222122222221221212 1112212  514408131771   2 121211
40111212125552222122222122221212122122121132661013311201152 221221
27110707124 622222112221222211122 2 12212  51661017 772  152 222211
46311919 24641222212222221211112311122 12 351641037157210152 221111
34110907124341222212222  1111231112221115 1551017377206252 211111
28110707525341122212222122221222411  11513 0616223204202 221211
43121111 21122122121222122222121251112221115244051332220 3302 122211
28110707 141112122212222221212222112    51551017177206302 221211
30110707325151511111112222212 2222111221222516508171572052 02 112111
26110202124451122112222112122112311122112231661037117205092 112111
    110808 641222212222211221122211 12    12314 061714 207052 221221
30110705323562222212222222111222511122121231660717267 1  2011221221
25212424 22 32222221222221 12221112     524405177771   1522221121
27310906323351222221222212222111124111221212525507261232082021112111
39310909123612122221221221211112111122121221520826232 1  2012111111
29110707126162212222222212 2222111222123426609371442081 52 211221
32110806325251221222221222211113112212115166 10717741   202211211t
23110302124431122122222122221112211122121351660817 1771  302 111121
24210201116141212222222122211211411122123351530 7271461  202 211111
30110302124352222222122122211 1 211122213352430715277205202 111111
25210303126131112222222222111111211112212235 16509462441  302 111111
42111313124321122212212222111211211112  225166091 4333203302 111211
24120303124532222221222221 22 2223122  11526508362771  092 221111
30110707525 122222122212222112231212221135 2550963566205102 111111
    11   123 41121122222    112225112    1152651044247205102 111111
32210808323631222221222122221222111122123451550916577205202 112111
28110605324351 222122221111 122231111222233 25510177771  1522112111
25110303 12 46222222122122211122311222 33515508277 54204202 112121
27110703326631222221121122221212311 2  1152440657775202202 112111
29110808124661222212222122212221222141 112221  526610174771  3022112111
302108081255322     211221122251212211 1 5 44082627720520212112 1
3111080132644 22222122222122122211112122 3352530717174205152 221221
47312222125 212       12221111121 11     1     122 121112
28110505224441222212121112211122311122122 23155073214420515121 12212
30110202116351212112222122221122311 2   1152650817377205302 2111112
```

```
28210404124422122222122212221112211112212335264091727620515222 11112
361118101244221222212222122111221111 2221  26610173662 07102 211212
29110707124342222221222222221112231112221 2252540717 57206152 211112
49112828 2466222222222111222212 22 2222221145141011372120130122 21222
3411131312666111111111111111111124112  23 24405271772043011112112
3311080512513121222122222211 1221111122213451661031177205452 112112
3531121211433212222122222212111 23111  3351550856224206152 112212
47111616125531212221221122211122311122 12 515509275661  302 112112
40111212 24 3122212112212211111  112222122516408 35151  252 11 212
3011080812522221222222221222111112112  24526309571611  152 112112
2411010112264 22222121222212122221112221125242037627 71  152 112  2
30111109124251222221222222211111241112212235164092727720 5152 112112
471123231211211222221212221112123112  11526610652572022012112212
303109094 566222222122221222212223111221212516610164321  152 111212
3411090912 241122221222222211111 23112  23516609464441  302 112112
333104041253511222211221222112223112  2451660915177205152 2121 2
33110303324331222221221122221112112121222133416610171771  152 111213
32111104124222221222221222112211511112221351550611 7771  102 1  3
30110909124522222221222221221111111122223516508174771  202 221213
38210908524541222212222221221122111122123152440415423 2082021112223
31110909124332222221222222212 12211112221225242071734 4206202 212223
28111010123461221122222122211121 3112  3252330257127204152 221213
2911040432536 22212222212211111212111221234 51540714 43206132 211213
29110505124562222122222221111223112  14115405165552012 02 221113
331101012445222211122222122 212 112  526610173772  202 221223
  312525 235421212222222221 1 2231112212 4514107171771  25222212 3
3221040452536221211122211222111131112221235 1661027377205202 1121 3
25110303124661222221212221211212111221224516608 16175204252 111113
242104041243512222221221222111121111122234 5144043757620 1302 111113
24210404124561221212221222211123122  3
2611050512345121212122212221 1111112  3441550957177207502 111213
291105051252611122212111212121121125111 2221335121022612220 14522111213
27110604126432222221222222212112231112 21223515307475751  302 221113
53112424125242222122222122221212111221233414 05 7471  302 121113
3411121212534122212222212222111114112  2131530632655202132 212113
29110507125531 2212122222111112123112  34524507357651  202 112113
34111212324251122221222221221112311112 22145  3
45111111125 2222222122122211112231112221345 16610111751  2 11 114
3811313116261222221221111111112111112221 234316410361571  152 111114
31110808122321222121222111111111221112212 52660924155205402 112114
441 181811634112212122222212122241112212 234166107171120430 2 121114
  11232312264122112122221221112 22 111221244526609151771  202 222214
32111111115321222221222212221122221221222 23516 0946266207302 111114
25320403223212222221222212211111111112  1660837776206302  11214
41211914 24451222221221222121112111122 21  514404123451  2 112214
24210303124242222221221122211112211122211 51661036265204102 122114
49112222115651222221222221212 22 111221213526608175571  302 112124
26110403123431222221222122 22 111411112221 2321530726235205202 1121 4
34110802125211222221222122211112111122212 3516408271661  202 112114
30110804425131211111221122211121 4112  12516605377771  252 1121 4
321111111126231222212221122211  121112212335153082726620815 22112114
```

```
24210404123341211111111112211112224111212234326408373562032O2 111115
38121515 2465112222112112221111221212212225165091 71771  2012211115
331111111221512221222221222112 2 1212212435165081 7177203152 221215
33111010 266422222212212221111124111222112515507263662051522112115
5111232312425222222221 212211112 112     2352550727 541   102 122225
351103031241612121212221221112221112     5255091 7777210302 211215
26110404125532221221221222111111212122133523 046554420820222111 15
44111515 2665112212222111212 1121112     52661017177201602 21215
37111414213222122122222222211111131112212235266101 71 7720140221111 15
44112121115651112222222222211111121112221125166101 71771  4022112115
34111212124351122222122122221122221112212345 5506272771  2022222215
4231181812212222112222222221111211222   21525508474541   2 111115
2811070712416121212222222222211111115122   44524306273771  152 112115
23110404325352222112221122221 1121112    135165091 4355207152 221215
41111919192535222212222121221111111 11222123314307263651  252 112115
37111507124341122212221 12222 1224111222133324408623222207182 111115
312102021253412221222211222112115112   2351661017177205072 112115
311105053266311          12221111111122  3451650411322207302 111115
5031292911535121212212211 21111121 11222122252640853 36 093512111115
26110501124651221121222122111 12222112   51330513254205 22111215
29110707125241222221122221111212211122213351550866263203202 122115
26110403115431222221222112111112 11122112352540917275204452 111115
5511303012565112212222122211112221111222113516509376572O8     21125
5411292912453112222221212212211 11 11122211221550837344205452 112115
50112525125431 222221 2221221111113112   2352530836166   252111 115
52111818126161122122222212211122112  1251661017177 01202 112125
47112222126651211222222112212212312  2351550825466205152 111215
    21262612          2221  2 2311         1            5
35110707115341222222122222111112311122213451530875177205351 2112115
28210505126462222122221 1221112222112   33515509173441  2012111115
50112525 152512111111121222111111112  4451 510175771  302211 115
35110808 24 312      2    11122511122213452550871 3761  2022112115
34111111125342221121222112111111211 1221223513304664771  202 221115
49112222125442212122222222211111111122   22515308142551  2022111215
27110505223632121211222212211211121 12   23515407264651  102 111115
32111010 24 32222221222221211112311 2  1252550824777207052 221215
351114141265312222212212221211112111222112512  0923174209301 111215
35111412125 322222212222122221 1251112211  51630833633205151 2222115
    11151422111222212222222121 12222112   24325 0811111201  22222225
45111616124632211112112122221121 51112212345233051 74771    11112115
42111818  56612211122221211112123111221 22342530417434204301 2221215
5011222212564122211222222221211 12 111212 151 5072547520430121 1125
44112020126352222221 2221222112223111212223516610377552052O2 1 1125
```

```
242203035242212221222221222211124111122233526609176772O5152 111214
383118043123412111221221221211112111221221325509361772O4302 112114
321113101243512122222221222121214111221212326309462771  252 112214
291104041152512212222222222111 2151112221335143O8171331  2O2 112214
363109091164611222221212221111111111122121321461O25111207152 111114
252102  126651211221221122211111 3112    3516608675771  452 112 14
241102023253312222221222222112  131112212233142O827267203252 112114
24110202 252311221212211122211 2251112212235165102737720415 2 111114
381111111233522222212222221211121111222124514440917377 1  452 221114
48112221125  221222212222211111121 11              1  2O2 111114
271106044242612222211221221 2 1123112     34316508261771  3O2 112114
39 115141255311222221222222111222511122 12 1515608265672O74O2 1111 4
28210707115261222221222221121221511 2     345265O91736720715 2 222214
221102025251612222221111222 1122511222121141440771765 1  2O12112115
25110303325352222122222112221111311122121252540753 55203201211 2215
242104043254611112212221111111 231122212  5166O917477208202 211115
35111111423342 2221222122212 2123112    335254O816266 1  2O2 221115
221104022253312222122211222112225112221211515508143521  15121222 25
371114143244612211222212221 2 111311122212352540917477205202 112115
311105051245411212222212122111 2 1112  12514407261661  2 111 15
321109091244412221211222121211123111222132524308275552O315 2 112215
291107061244522221222222221211111131112221125165O72736620525 2 112115
232102024231111222212211222212223112    1451660855555205152 221215
313110101245522222212221222121121111222122515507364562O52O2 111115
363104044152512221221222121121121111221135166101433420620222 11 2215
411106051231422222121221221121123112  1161650817474201202 112115
333104011246611222212212222111111111122123151661O14177205202 112215
241205042234411221212111221112221 2  13425306361441  3O2 2 1115
        1232221222222122 221251112212323 24 O811177201  21212125
291104041243522222212221222212 22 112  1152550817177201152 221215
242101011256311221222222221211122111221223515507362651  152 111115
26210606425 6112111122212211122251112122  52550817 77201102 221115
212102021246522221222112221122241 2    2152660971176205  2 221215
263107045253512221222221222112223112  1452550817777201202 221215
421114123243522212222222221211221111221234514307574661  15121111 15
33111010 26112222221222221211112411122 12 5265O81727720520121 12215
311110101234611221222221122221112311 2  1452541O166772081512112215
311108081242422122222222211111211212212445144081717720520121 12125
361110104 24 612222212221222112221112212445264O917377207402 121215
381117173154522222211222221122112 111222123525508264771  301222112 5
321110101245522222212221212211111211122124452660974256206202 111215
2611030312424 22222212122211112 1 112  52330515 751  3O2 1111 5
361111O952653122222212221211122 2 112  1352541011342204152 22112 5
47111515 26161222221122222212222211122 1 4526610174  207151222111 5
301104044251412222211221221111122111222122525307166661  2O11221215
411118181254412222221122211112211222113215508775741  2O12211215
311110101151212212222211222212223111221222516610143332O72012221115
34111313124251212222222212221121131112212245162O8271371  2O1 11 115
261103034254212222221212222 11 221112    52551O171771  4011211215
33110707315 31212221221122 2 11111111112212 51 506271 77  152 112115
271208O12154422222212221222111114112    2352660926364 1  1O2 112115
```

DISPLAY A4

```
TITLE NAME 'POLICE PERCEPTIONS STUDY'
DATA LIST   RECORDS=1 NOTABLE
       /1 AGE 1-2 MARSTAT 3 SEX 4  YRSLAWEN 5-6
          YRSPOLIC 7-8 FATHEDUC 9 CAMEFROM 10 PARTMAR 11
          POLRESPD 12 REPEAT 13
          INCREASE 14 PUNDETER 15 SSA 16 FILECOMP 17
          PRESCHAR 18 MOVEOUT 19 LEVTEMP 20 FRIENDS 21
          INJUNC 22 INJEFFEC 23 MEDIATOR 24 COUNCEL 25
          BREKAPAR 26 BOTHPART 27 ARREST 28 OFTARRES 29
          TEAMS 30 BETTERWA 31 SWACCOMP 32 DIFFEREN 33
          DOSOWORK 34 MORETIME 35 DISTINCT 36
          KNOWLAW 37 PUBOPIN 38 PEREXPER 39 TYPEDIFF 40
          NOWEAPON 41 WOWAITS 42 WOPRECHAR 43 CORRABUS 44
          DRINKING 45 DRUNK 46 INFLU 47-48 RETURNS 49
          REGRET 50 DIVORCES 51 ONERELA 52
          SEPSTOP 53 PUBSUPP 54 RANKSUPP 55-56
          LENGMIN 57-58 ALONE 59 COMFORT 60
          NEEDTRAI 61 WORKSHOP 62 TRNSUFF 63 TRNLENG 64
          SHELTER 65 CITY 66
SET BLANKS=999
RECODE PUNDETER CAMEFROM(5=999)
RECODE DIVORCES(0=999)
MISSING VALUES ALL(999)
BEGIN DATA
enter raw data here
END DATA
enter procedure statements here
FINISH
/*
```

APPENDIX B

ADC STUDY

This appendix contains the data collection instrument, raw data,
and variable organization sheets from the study of the economic, health,
and social effects on families cut from the Aid to Families with
Dependent Children program. The study was conducted by the Iowa School
of Social Work Research Center directed by John Craft.

The questionnaire and data used here are a condensed version of the
orginal instrument and data. Two hundred respondents were interviewed,
but the results of just 75 are presented here.

Display B1 presents the condensed version of the telephone
interview instrument.

Display B2 presents the Coding Organization Form that identifies
variable number, variable name, data in columns, measurement level, and
category codes.

Display B3 presents the raw data. Each case contains three lines.

141

DISPLAY B1

ADC Telephone Interview Instrument

1. What is your birthdate?

2. What is the last year of school you completed?

3. When you were growing up, did your family ever receive ADC benefits?

4. What do you think was the most important benefit of ADC to you?

5. Why did you first go on ADC? (Interviewer may select more than one category and use space here to describe).

6. Think back to the time when you were cut from ADC, how serious did you think it would be? Did it present an extremely serious problem for you, a somewhat serious problem, or was it not a serious problem for you?

7. Would you enroll in ADC again?

8. How do you feel about the cut today?

9. What have been the benefits of being dropped from ADC? Were there positive things?

10. What have been the losses of being dropped from ADC? Were there any negative things?

11. What do you think has been the effect of the cut on your children?

12. What is your total income now?

13. What was your income before the cut?

14. What are your total expenses now?

15. What were your major expenses before the cut?

16. In the past year have you:

    a. Had your mortgage forclosed?

    b. Been evicted for failure to pay your rent?

    c. Had your phone cut off?

    d. Had your gas or electricity shut off?

    e. Had any furniture or appliances repossessed?

    f. Had your car repossessed?

    g. Had any credit cards recalled?

    h. Had any bills referred to collection agencies?

17. Are you able to do any of the following things to save

    money? And do you do these things more than before you were

    dropped from ADC, less than before, or about the same?

    a. Exchange babysitting with friends or family.

    b. Pawned items for cash.

    c. Have a home food garden for fresh, frozen, or canned vegetables.

    d. Receive government cheese or butter.

    e. Shopped at food co-ops, other discount food stores, or belong to

    a food club.

    f. Rely on used clothes for the family.

18. At the time you were cut from ADC, did you consider quitting your

    job so you could stay on ADC?

19. Did you think about reducing the numbers of hours you were

    working to stay on ADC?

20. Does someone else take care of your children on a regular basis now?

21. Who provides your child care?

22. How many hours per week do you have someone care for your children while you work?

23. What are the reasons you use child care?

24. Do you receive (Title XX) day care assistance?

25. What time of day do you use child care?

26. Did someone provide childcare in Sep 81 (when cut)?

   a. If yes, who provided the childcare and how much did it cost?

27. Do you have health insurance?

28. What kind of health insurance do you have?

29. Do you or any members of your family have a major or persistant medical problem?

30. How frequently do you and your family see a health practitioner (doctor, home health agency, chiropractic)? Which and how often?

31. Do you think you go to doctor more often, less often, or about the same as when you were cut from ADC?

32. Do you have dental insurance for your family?

33. Do you think you go to dentist more often, less often, or about the same as when you were cut from ADC?

34. Do you feel that your children get enough to eat now?

35. Did you ever miss a meal because you didn't have enough food?

36. Do your children receive free lunches in school?

37. Do your children receive reduced-price lunches in school?

38. Has the quality of your food changed since you were cut? Would you say the quality is higher, about the same, or lower?

39. Did you move after you were cut?

40. Did you move one year before you were cut?

41. How many times have you moved?

42. Did you move because of the cut?

43. Why did you move because of the cut?

44. Overall, how would you compare your family's life situation today with the way it was when you were cut? Would you say that things are better, the same, or that they are worse?

45. I'm going to read a list of things that have happened to many people since they were cut. Can you tell me if any of the following have happened to you?

a. Need emergency medical care?

b. Been a victim of a crime?

c. Someone in family got in trouble with police?

d. Had a furnace, refrigerator, or other major appliance break down?

e. Had something like a car or furnature repossessed?

f. Had someone close to you die?

g. Had to go to court?

h. Had a child born to a teenage daughter?

i. Had a child run away?

j. Experienced drug or alcohol abuse?

k. Was separated or divorced?

l. Became married?

m. Someone in the family was arrested?

n. Someone in the family had major illness?

o. Experienced any other major event, good, or bad?

46. Have any of the following things happened to your children?

a. Had problems that required your going to school for a special conference?

b. Been referred to a school psychologist or social worker?

c. Been suspended or sent home from school?

d. Started working (probe)?

e. Been arrested?

f. Been in detention or jail?

g. Been in juvenile court?

h. Received a special award?

i. Been sent to a special or alternative school?

j. Been sent to an institution (probe)?

k. Been a victim of a crime by someone else?

m. Been sent to a foster home (probe)?

47. Do you believe any of the events you just described were caused by being dropped from ADC? If yes, which ones?

48. If you would like to see some changes in your life, what would they be?

49. Given the way your life is right now, would your say that you are in control of things, things are in control of you, or you and things are seeing eye to eye?

50. Some people worry more than others. Would you say you never worry, worry a little, worry a lot, or worry all the time?

51. How do you feel about your relationship with your children? Would you say things are great, could be better, or there is a lot of tension?

DISPLAY B2

Coding Organization Form
ADC Study

Variable No.	Variable Name	Data In Column(s)	Measurement Level	Category Codes
1	MAGE	1-2	I	00-99
2	ED	3-4	I	06-20
3	HIST	5	N	0=NO,1=YES
4	ADCBEN	6	N	1=MONEY 2=MEDICAID 3=BOTH
5	WHYADC	7-8	N	01=DIVORCE 02=DEATH/SPOUSE 03=SEPARATION 04=NOT MARRIED, BIRTH/CHILD 05=LAID OFF WORK 06 TO 99=OTHER
6	SERIOUS	9	O	1=EXTREMELY 2=SOMEWHAT 3=NOT SERIOUS
7	ENROLL	10	N	0=NO,1=YES, 2=LAST RESORT
8	FEEL	11	N	1=POSITIVE 2=NEGATIVE 3=NEUTRAL 4=NO OPINION
9A-9C	BEN1-BEN3	12-17	N	01=INDEPENDENCE 02=FAMILY CLOSER 03=LEARN/BUDGET 04=FREE/DSS 05=NONE 06=GO/SCHOOL 07-99=OTHER
10A-10C	LOSS1-LOSS3	18-23	N	01=MEDICAL/DENTAL 02=NEG RE: ADC 03=LESS TIME/FAMILY 04=LOST MONEY 05=LOST INDEPENDENCE 06=QUIT JOB 07=DIVORCE/SEP 08=FAMILY STRESS 09-99=OTHER

11A-11C	CE1 TO CE3	24-29	N	01=TOO YOUNG
				02=NONE
				03=LESS TIME FOR
				CHILDREN
				04=LEARN VALUE $$
				05-99=OTHER
12	TOTINC	30-34	I	0-99,999
13	TOTINCB	35-39	I	0-99,999
14	TOTEXP	40-44	I	0-99,999
15	TOTEXPB	45-49	I	0-99,999
16	FP1-FP8	50-57	N	0=NO,1=YES
17	SM1-SM6	58-63	N	0=NO,1=MORE,
				2=SAME,3=LESS
18	QUIT	64	N	0=NO,1=YES
19	REDUCE	65	N	0=NO,1=YES

LINE 2

20	CCNOW	1	N	0=NO,1=YES
21	CCWHO	2-3	N	01=MOTHER
				02=SISTER
				03=OTHER/REL
				04=FRIEND
				05=LIC DAYCARE
				06=NURSERY SCHOOL
				07=SITTER IN HOME
				08=SITTER OUT HOME
				09-99=OTHER
22	CCHR	4-5	I	00-99
23	PRIMUSE	6-7	N	01=WORK
				02=JOB SEARCH
				03=SCHOOL
				04=HEALTH
				05=CHILD NEEDS
				06=ODD WORK HOURS
				07=PROTECTIVE
				SERVICE ORDER
				08=CHILD DEV
				09=OTHER
24	XX	8	N	0=NO,1=YES
25	T1-T2	9-12	N	01=DAY
				02=HALF DAY
				03=BEFORE SCHOOL
				04=AFTER SCHOOL
				05=EARLY EVE
				06=ALL EVENING
				07=WEEKEND DAYS
				08=WEEKEND EVES
				09=OTHER
26	BCCUSE	13	N	0=NO,1=YES
26	BCCWHO	14-15	N	(SEE CCWHO ABOVE)

26	BCCAMT	16-18	I	0-999
27	HEALTH	19	N	0=NO,1=YES
28	KIND	20-21	N	01=MEDICAID
				02=PRIVATE
				03=LOW INCOME
				CLINIC
				04=OTHER
29	CHRONIC	22	N	0=NO,1=YES
30	HFREQ	23-24	I	0-99
31	HCHA	25	N	1=MORE,2=SAME
				3=LESS,4=DON'T KNOW
32	DENINS	26	N	0=NO,1=YES
33	DENCHA	27	N	1=MORE,2=SAME
34	ENOUGH	28	N	0=NO,1=YES
35	MSMEAL	29	N	0=NO,1=YES
36	FREE	30	N	0=NO,1=YES
37	REDML	31	N	0=NO,1=YES
38	QUAL	32	N	1=HI,2=SAME,3=LOW
39	AMOVE	33	N	0=NO,1=YES
40	BMOVE	34	N	0=NO,1=YES
41	NUMMOVE	35	I	0-9
42	RELCUT	36	N	0=NO,1=YES
				3=LESS,4=DON'T KNOW
43	RELWHY	37	N	01=EVICTED
				02=CHEAPER RENT
				03=BETTER HOME
				04=OTHER
44	LIFE	39	N	1=BETTER,2=SAME
				3=WORSE

LINE 3

45	EV1 TO EV15	1-15	N	0=NO,1=YES
46	CEV1-CEV12	16-27	N	0=NO,1=YES
47	EVADC	28	N	0=NO,1=YES
48	LF1-LF3	29-34	N	01=EDUCATION
				02=MORE MONEY
				03=NEW HOME
				04=GET JOB
				05-99=OTHER

49	TOP	35	N	1=IN CONTROL,
				2=NO CONTROL,
				3=IN/OUT CONTROL
50	WORRY	36	N	1=NEVER WORRY
				2=WORRY/LITTLE
				3=WORRY A LOT
				4=WORRY ALL/TIME
51	RELATE	37	N	1=GREAT
				2=COULD BE BETTER
				3=LOT/TENSION

DISPLAY B3

ADC STUDY RAW DATA

```
381401 1201 1 0 0 1 0 0 2075  700  834  5500000000000201211
0 0 0 00 0 00 0   01 21 2303100020000 01
1101000001010011001000100110010011 0 0131
261202 7112 5 0 0 1  412  273 9700  629  3900000000000201222
0 0 0 00 0 00 0   00 0112300101330000 03
11010110000001100000000000001 4 8 0321
351202 1112 1 0 0 1 6 0  445  565  803  3320000000100010022
1 1 5 10 2 01 1 500 00 1200101331010 03
0001000000000000010000000000 2 1 4231
26 902 5211 1 0 0 1 0 0  631  525  623   00000000120200012
1 1 5 20 3 01 1   01 21 2100100020000 02
100101000000010000000000000000 6 0 0331
281602 1212 4 0 0 4 0 0  502  724  740  4890000000020200222
1 840 10 1 01 01251 20 2200100020000 02
00000000000000100000000000000 4 0 0121
 0 902 1112 5 0 0 1 3 4  574  664  634  4201000001121011211
0 0 0 00 0 01 0 600 01 0300111331011 11
000000110000001000000001000001111213332
391201 8112 1 0 0 4 0 0  624  680 1046  5382000000100001011
3 0 0 00 0 01 01201 00 1300111330000 03
00000000000000110000001000000 2 0 0243
291202 4124 5 0 0 1 0 0  680 1090  942  6600000000020212222
1 130 10 5 01 11000 01 4200111320000 02
01010000000000011100000000100 3 4 2342
361303 4124 2 0 0 1 0 0  806  750 1110  5550000000000103211
1 0 0 10 1 01 01501 20 4200103330000 01
11010100000000010110000000000 1 2 0342
291202 1203 1 4 0 1 4 0  356  365  449  3160000000022111122
1 110 10 7 01 1   00 00 6300111330000 02
101101100000111000010110000 2 4 5233
341202 1122 1 4 5 1 3 4  819  512  352  2052000000000212022
0 0 0 00 0 00 0   00 00 1300101320000 02
0001000000000000001000010000 3 4 6231
401211 5112 5 0 0 4 0 0  442  442  420  1500000000000012122
0 0 0 00 0 01 01000 0012200103120000 01
000000000000000000000000000 2 5 0121
291212 5113 1 0 0 1 8 0  877  667  768  4350000000110001122
1 2 5 10 5 01 01501 2177200113121143 23
100001000000000100000000000 1 6 0343
351202 4112 4 0 0 1 4 0  531  776  561  2900010001120012112
1 140 10 6 81 01201 20 1300101020000 01
01010010000000000001000000000 1 2 3221
351203 1112 5 0 0 4 0 0 1519 1438 1113  3250000000000202233
0 0 0 00 0 00 0   01 2124100100031020 03
0001010000000011100000010000 21213232
291201 5112 1 0 0 4 1 9  852  916  509  4580000000010211111
1 140 10 1 01 01721 21 2200100021010 03
```

```
1001000000000010100000000000 2 5 0122
431402 7122 1 2 0 112 0   680   570   404  35000000000020110111
1 132 10 6 01 1   00 00 1300103130000 02
1001010101000000100000000000 2 0 0241
221102 1212 5 0 0 1 2 8  460   505   200  31000000000020010022
3 0 0 01 0 01 0 800 00 1200101321131 23
1000010000000000000000000000001213 0232
321602 5212 1 4 0 1 0 0   538   510   307  12500000000000211122
1 188 00 0 01 08881 21 1300101330000 03
01000000000101100000000000000 6 0 0322
39140214222 1 0 0 1 2 4   820   935   781  46500200000000103222
1 4 0 11 9 01 01250 00 1300113130000 02
1001010011000001101000010000 1 2 0322
35130214000 4 0 0 1 412   692   654   642  41700000000122112211
0 0 0 00 0 00 0  00 00 0000000000000 03
1011011000010101101010100000 213 0332
371202 1112 5 0 0 8 0 0   684   706   718  56800000000000222222
0 0 0 00 0 01 01721 21 2212013130000 03
11110010011100111000000000001 0 0 0243
241202 0212 1 0 0 4 0 0   625   854   499  37500000000000011111
1 725 10 1 01 81001 20 4212100030341 43
1000000000000000000000000000 2 0 0231
281202 5222 5 0 0 4 1 0   787   868   716  57020000000020000022
1 535 10 1 71 51501 20 1212100020000 02
1000000000000000000000000000 6 2 0232
411203 1112 0 0 0 1 3 0   674   864   643  38600100000100303122
088 0 00 0 01 81851 21 4202010031123 93
10110100010011111111100100010112 0 0243
39120214222 1 0 0 4 0 0   570   730   793  49100000000000213222
1 1 0 10 3 41101081 2110202104130000 02
1001010000000100000000000000 21213321
431203 4312 0 0 0 1 4 0   438 1137   692  49400000000000110222
088 0 00 0 00 0  01 11 9212111320000 02
0001000100000000000000000100 6 0 0321
431202 6223 5 0 0 112 4 1129   843   767  43400000000000210233
088 0 00 0 00 0  01 10 1303101321121 11
00000010001000000000000000011 0 0331
291303 3122 0 0 0 1 412     0   417   507  24500000000010310133
1 840 30 1 01 8 601 20 2303000020000 01
0001000000000100000000000000 4 0 0332
21130111323 1 0 0 0 0 0   382   300   440  21320100001000011212
088 0 00 0 01 11401 10 6313000021021 21
10000110000000000000000000010 4 7 0131
361201 1213 0 0 0 1 8 0 2064   380   658  35300110001000022233
088 0 00 0 00 0  01 21 4212103120000 03
1000011001001111010000100000 1 2 0332
56 812 5112 0 0 0 1 812   160   807   580  34200000001002220112
088 0 00 0 00 0  00 01 2202101320000 03
0000000000000001100000100000 8 0 0331
34 80214112 0 0 0 1 0 0   328   592   623  42200010001000010122
088 0 00 0 01 2 860 00 1232111330000 02
```

```
000000000000000001000000000000 612 0232
311202 5112 0 0 0 1 0 0   477   570   467   110000000000210021
1 160 10 1 71 1 601 20 1202100020000 02
100101000000000000000010000012 0 0231
25 902 1122 1 0 0 3 8 0   852   695   391   4232010000002101121
088 0 00 0 01 51081 11 3212101321010 03
001000110001001101000000000001702041213
251200 5102 1 0 0 1 4 8   560   650   642   1750000000100000012
1 215 10 3 41 5 501 21 4303100031130 02
000000000000000000000000000000 2 312000
231412 5122 0 0 0 1 4 0   565   780   635   4080111000120010112
1 130 10 1 01 41291 20 6112111331121 11
000001000000010000000000000102120 2420
251202 5212 4 0 0 1 4 0   495   666   516   3240000000010010222
1 840 10 1 01 81081 20 2103100020000 02
001010000001100000000000000001140 0 2320
331201 4112 0 0 0 1 212   556   679   756   5100000000000000011121
1 423 10 1 71 81290 00 2203011320110 03
000001000010000110001000000 2 0 0332
27 912 5222 0 0 0 1 4 8   546   533   648   4690000000000000111122
0 0 0 00 0 01 81940 01 3303111321010 03
100100000100000000000000000 2 4 0131
36130311112 1 0 0 1 0 0   700   650   549   3600000000010001122
1 836 10 6 01 81401 21 4203000030000 00
100100000000001100000000000 2 512231
42 801 4202 0 0 0 1 0 0   438   521   501   4252010000100112222
0 0 0 00 0 00 0  00 01 3203111331020 01
100100000000000001010000000 212 0241
291302 4121 1 0 0 4 0 0   842   810   583   3760000000010110211
1 820 10 3 41 81201 2112301111320000 02
100100000000011100000100000 1 2 6132
281302 9222 3 0 0 1 4 0   546   722   641   4912002000120010022
0 0 0 00 0 01 81081 20 2212101321010 02
000000000000000000000000000000 412 0132
291202 4201 1 4 5 1 0 0   602   534   607   3600000000020202022
1 3 5 10 3 00 0  01 20 1202100021010 02
000000000001000100000000000011 0 0321
251402 5323 1 0 0 2 0 0   528   766   460   2802000000030110122
1 845 10 1 01 81201 20 4102100030110 01
000000000000001000000000000001 6 0 0332
301202 1222 1 4 0 1 0 0   727   886   788   5160000000010101222
0 0 0 00 0 01 92580 0112303110030000 01
100110000000010100000000000011213 0331
27 311 5323 1 0 0 1 0 0 1052     0     0   00000000120011222
0 0 0 00 0 01 82150 00 4102111311120 00
000000000000000000000000000 0 0 0000
371202 3213 2 0 0 1 0 0   957   331   567   01002000100220222
0 0 0 00 0 00 0  01 2112303103120000 03
001101000000101000001000001 0 0 0232
471202 1201 1 0 0 1 0 0   560   221   533   1940000000000001222
0 0 0 00 0 00 0  01 20 4303100020000 01
```

```
100000000000001000100010000   2 0 0321
301401 1312 4 0 0 4 0 0   542      0  722   5190001000000110122
1 714 10 6 01 82151 1012212111330000 03
0000010000000000000000000000   212 0242
241402 5112 1 0 0 1 2 4  710   800   621   4150000000000212212
1 735 10 6 01 51721 2010313104420000 03
1101000000000000000000000001   812 0232
341202 1303 1 4 0 1 312   816  1089  881   3470000000020001121
541 450012 60 1 410 1731000010030000 01
0001001000000101100000000000   2 512311
26130114112 5 0 0 1 4 0   970   731  851   4400001000102020022
1 8 5 10 1 01 81721 21 2112104420000 02
1000010000000000000000000000   2 0 0321
421202 3122 1 0 0 110 0   702  1556  760   3800000000000001122
0 0 0 00 0 00 0   01 2012203101320000 02
0000000000000000000000000012 0 0321
221202 5112 1 2 0 1 4 0   476   476  223   1830000000010000122
0 0 0 01 0 01 48881 1088211101330000 03
0001000000000000000000000000   1 0 0331
331202 1122 1 0 0 1 0 0   869   603  814   4800000000000021222
1 140 10 1 01 1  01 21 4303103020000 01
1100000000000001110000000000   212 0243
421201 0000 0 0 0 0 0 0   810   467  439   1940000000000001122
0 0 0 00 0 01 1   01 21 4203103010000 02
0001000000000000100000000000   2 0 0331
271202 1113 1 0 0 1 0 0   817   825  518   4650000000100101312
1 548 10 1 01 51301 2177302103121130 01
0000000001000010000000000000   2 0 0122
311303 1313 0 0 0 1 0 0   789   799  693   2900000000000222020
0 0 0 00 0 01 7 601 1177212101320000 02
1001010000010101000000010000012 0 0321
301202 5223 1 0 0 112 0   700   730  591   2350000000110001111
1 540 10 1 01 81291 2077303110030110 02
0000011000000000000000000001   2 4 0231
31 302 5312 1 0 0 1 0 0   640   528  637   4480000000032000022
1 340 10 1 01 81501 2077313013110000 02
1001000000000001000000100000   2 0 0241
401401 1214 1 0 0 0 112   601   581  260   1200000000000010200
0 0 0 00 0 00 0   01 1124212101330000 02
1000010000000110001000100000 1213 0242
 01002 7112 0 0 0 1 4 0   618   619  529   3560010000100111121
0 0 0 00 0 01 8 431 1112113111330000 03
00010000001100011000001000011,1213 0231
421202 4112 1 5 0 1 4 0  1007   689  921   5910011000100010212
0 0 0 00 0 00 0   01 2112313101330110 01
10010101000001011000011000011 1 0 0343
281202 4113 1 0 0 1 0 0  1333   360  660   3360000000000222222
0 0 0 00 0 00 0   01 20 1202103120000 01
0001001000000001000000000000012 0 0341
33140114122 0 0 0 0 1 4   971  1110  779   3370000000000120200
0 0 0 00 0 00 0   00 0124303111330000 03
```

```
100101000000010100100010000000 2 0 0331
461202 3311 0 0 0 1 0 0  680  591  619  3040000000000000000222
0 0 0 00 0 00 0  01 20 1202103121010 01
000000100000000000100000000011 0 0322
291112 1112 0 0 0 1 4 5  482  812  115  29301110001211111112
1 315 30 5 01 3  01 10 2212111321020 03
100000000000000100000000100001 412 0221
34120388112 0 0 0 1 4 0  445  689  628  5300000000120010022
1 8 8 10 7 01 81404 0177203103120000 03
010000000000001000000000000000 2 6 0332
36120113112 0 0 0 1 3 4  672  989  643  5980010000110111111
1 560 11 1 01 52801 21 6203011330000 03
101101101100101110010110011 11213333
291102 4113 4 0 0 1 412  419  774  731  4000011000000110222
1 445 10 4 61 81501 2012202111321010 02
100101100010001000000000100000 21213322
301608 1122 4 0 0 1 4 0  810  850  514  3550000000000000000122
1 148 60 9 01 11301 20 5312100011020 02
100000000000000000000010000012 0 0131
381202 5213 0 0 0 1 0 0  450 1033  403  2110000000010110122
1 110 10 6 01 8 861 11 6312001310000 02
000101000000100000000100000 4 0 0122
301202 5118 1 0 0 1 4 0  588  618  437  2640000000010211022
1 7 5 10 3 41 7 251 20 2302103130000 01
000001000000000000000000000000 2 6 0131
```

CODING SHEET AND ORGANIZATION FORM

Coding Organization Form

ADC Study

_____

Variable number	Variable name	Data in column(s)	Measurement level	Category codes
_____	_____	_____	_____	_____
_____	_____	_____	_____	_____
_____	_____	_____	_____	_____
_____	_____	_____	_____	_____
_____	_____	_____	_____	_____
_____	_____	_____	_____	_____
_____	_____	_____	_____	_____
_____	_____	_____	_____	_____
_____	_____	_____	_____	_____
_____	_____	_____	_____	_____
_____	_____	_____	_____	_____
_____	_____	_____	_____	_____
_____	_____	_____	_____	_____
_____	_____	_____	_____	_____
_____	_____	_____	_____	_____

Index

THE BOOK MANUFACTURE

Statistics and Data Analysis for Social Workers was typeset by Professional Services, Champaign, IL. It was printed and bound at Kingsport Press, Kingsport, Tennessee. Cover design was by Jane Rae Brown. Internal design was by the F.E. Peacock Publishers' art department. The typeface is Times Roman with Helvetica display.